Hot Sexplay for your Weekend Away

Text © 2010 Michele Zipp
Photography © 2010 Quiver

First published in the USA in 2009 by
Quiver, a member of
Quayside Publishing Group
100 Cummings Center
Suite 406-L
Beverly, MA 01915-6101
www.quiverbooks.com

The Publisher maintains the records relating to images in this book
required by 18 USC 2257. Records are located at Rockport Publishers, Inc.,
100 Cummings Center, Suite 406-L, Beverly, MA 01915-6101.

12 11 10 09 08 1 2 3 4 5

ISBN-13: 978-1-59233-326-4
ISBN-10: 1-59233-326-5

Library of Congress Cataloging-in-Publication Data
Zipp, Michele.
  Hot sexplay for your weekend away : erotic interactions, inspirations,
massages, and positions to have the weekend vacation of your dreams / Michele Zipp.
     p. cm.
  ISBN-13: 978-1-59233-326-4
  ISBN-10: 1-59233-326-5
  1. Sex instruction. 2. Sex. 3. Erotica. I. Title.
  HQ31.Z67 2008
  613.9'6—dc22
                                                                    2008032990

Cover design by Traffic Design Consultants
Photography by Jacques Seurat except for the following: gettyimages.com: pages 5,
6, 8, 11, 15, 104; istockphoto.com: pages 4, 5, 15, 22, 25, 26, 36, 50, 52, 56, 69, 90,
92, 95, 104, 107, 111, 118, 121, 125, 130, 133, 136; masterfile.com: pages 8, 11;
and shutterstock.com: pages 4, 66.

Printed and bound in Singapore

Hot Sexplay for your Weekend Away

playful erotic interactions, inspirations,
massages and positions for the weekend
vacation of your dreams

Michele Zipp

Former Editor-in-Chief

Playgirl Magazine

QUIVER

Wanderlust: The Great Escape!

This book is about lust: both romantic lust, the erotic longing you feel for your lover, and wanderlust, the urge to escape your everyday life, see and experience new places, and find adventure.

Hot Sexplay for Your Weekend Away focuses on both, serving up ten sex-themed two-night adventures that can help inject new passion, romance, or intimacy into your sex life. Whether you're seeking an erotic experience outside your comfort zone, such as a ménage à trios, or just looking for a destination to act out a fantasy, unleash your inner vixen, or make love in a different setting, this book is for you!

I will show you how to inject your relationship with a much-needed dose of sizzling eroticism—the type of triple-X passion most people only fantasize about. Each chapter covers everything: how to plan, what to pack, what to do Friday (or your first day), what to do Saturday (or your second day), and some extra special techniques for exciting sex! The sexy adventures outlined in this book will help you:

- Seek out destinations and research where to go.

- Learn new approaches to foreplay, intimacy, and lovemaking.

- Read success stories from other adventurous couples.

- Explore new erotic and sensual activities.

- Take advantage of your surroundings to sex up your trip.

- Create memories and experiences to reuse at home.

No matter what your budget, time frame, or reason for needing a getaway, there's a titillating vacation here tailored just for you. So get packing—and get ready for fun!

—Michele Zipp

"A happy gardener is one with dirty fingernails, and a happy cook is a fat cook. I never get tired of what I do because I'm a sex fiend."
—John Curtis Estes (a.k.a. John Holmes), American porn star

Chapter 1:
PORN STAR WANNABE

If you've always fantasized about the glamour, the attention, and the sexy lifestyle that a porn star lives, then this is your chance to experience it firsthand. Not only will you travel in the style of a movie star, but you'll also dress and act the part, pamper each other like only Hollywood actors and actresses can, and star in a porn movie of your own making!

Planning Your Getaway

First things first—you need a destination. If you can't afford a trip to Hollywood, go for glamour (where you'll be pampered like a star) or a small town (where you can be anonymous OR make a scene the locals will never forget!). Check out these ideas and resources for planning your porn star adventure, and be sure to book your hotel ahead of time.

- Book a luxury hotel using a website such as www.luxuryhoteladvisor.com or locate a B&B in an off-the-beaten-track destination using www.bnbfinder.com or www.bbonline.com.

- Want to take some inspiration from real porn stars? Consider booking a trip to Las Vegas around the time of the Adult Entertainment Expo, the official trade show of the porn industry. You can even enter a contest for the best booty, the hottest fan, or the best on-stage orgasm! Visit http://show.adultentertain mentexpo.com for more information.

- Las Vegas too far? Visit www.thefloatingworld.com/events.html for year-round adult entertainment and porn industry events, awards, and expos closer to home.

- Visit www.spafinder.com to locate a spa near you or select a destination based on the treatment you're looking for.

Packing for Pleasure

In addition to your getaway clothes and toiletries, don't forget to pack some key props for your sexplay and movie making:

- Dress clothes for him (e.g., suit jacket and pants, tie, button-down shirt, etc.)

- Pajamas for him, preferably silk

- Dress clothes for her (e.g., day dress, slip dress for evening, high heels, etc.)

- Sheer sexy nightie or new lingerie for her

- Massage oil

- Video camera, extra batteries, and tripod

- Vibrator and extra batteries

- Other sex toys as desired

Friday

WHAT'S IN A NAME?

If you're going to play porn star, you need a sexy name to use for the weekend! So make one up on the way to your destination:

- Play a game: Use the first pet you had as your first name and the first street you lived on as your surname (e.g., Cody Duncan, Sugar Stonecleave, etc.).

- Borrow from others: Take a well-known name, such as Linda Lovelace, and make it your own.

- Play with alliteration or rhymes: How about Handy Andy, Pamela Pussy, or Chrissie Comes?

- Use a play on words such as Rusty Gadget, Spread Eagle, Hugh G. Rection, and so on.

"SOME MOVIE STARS WEAR THEIR SUNGLASSES EVEN IN CHURCH. THEY'RE AFRAID GOD MIGHT RECOGNIZE THEM AND ASK FOR AUTOGRAPHS."

—FRED ALLEN, AMERICAN COMEDIAN

STUDY THE CLASSICS

This group of classic porn movies date back to the 1970s, which is considered the "Golden Age of Porn." Tonight, rent one of these oldies but goodies for some classic inspiration. Imagine recreating a scene that you like, or use one of these films as a springboard for your own improvisation!

Deep Throat (starring Linda Lovelace). Although Linda has an active and energetic sex life, she's unsatisfied. Her frustration leads her to seek medical help; fortunately, the doctor explains the problem: her clitoris is mistakenly located at the back of her throat! Naturally, there's a very simple remedy, which the doctor, as well as various other men, proceed to demonstrate.

Behind the Green Door (starring Marilyn Chambers). The movie tells the story of Gloria (played by Chambers), a woman who is kidnapped and blindfolded. When her blindfold is removed, she finds herself on a stage in front of masked men. A series of women, followed by men, make love to her while the audience progressively moves into an orgy. The story is told as a flashback from a man in the audience.

The Opening of Misty Beethoven (starring Constance Money). This is a pornographic take off on *My Fair Lady*. Misty (played by Money) replaces Eliza Doolittle, the flower girl in need of speech lessons, and Seymour Love (played by Jamie Gills) replaces Henry Higgins, the gentleman who wants to turn her into a lady. In this version, Seymour, a sophisticated sexologist, wants to turn Misty, a prostitute, into a goddess of passion. Seymour trains Misty for her big test—seducing a homosexual artist—but in the end she ends up falling for him.

Emmanuelle (starring Sylvia Kristel). France's contribution to skin flicks, *Emmanuelle* is a notorious X-rated classic about a diplomat's wife who is bored in Bangkok (and doesn't take up knitting). The film includes a variety of sex-related activities, including a noted scene in which a dancer inserts a cigarette into her vagina.

FEMALE FLUFFER ROLE-PLAY

In the porn industry, a fluffer is a hired member of the crew whose job is to sexually arouse the male participants for scenes where the man needs an erection. Tonight's game: to play fluffer with your porn star wannabe using massage oil, remembering that your job is to arouse your lover, but not bring him to orgasm!

Start by turning on some soft music, turning down the lights and/or lighting some candles, and letting your lover slip into a warm robe and slippers and sip a glass of wine while you create a soft and cozy surface using towels or blankets on your bed. Then try these massage ideas to get him ready for filming his scene.

Have your lover lie face up on the bed. Warm the massage oil in your hands, then use both your hands on his chest, gently working from the shoulders downward. Whisper that his penis is so beautiful, you can't wait to see it in action. Use smooth,

"MY REACTION TO PORN FILMS IS AS FOLLOWS: AFTER THE FIRST TEN MINUTES, I WANT TO GO HOME AND SCREW. AFTER THE FIRST 20 MINUTES, I NEVER WANT TO SCREW AGAIN AS LONG AS I LIVE."

—ERICA JONG, *PLAYBOY MAGAZINE*, SEPTEMBER 1975

continuous motions and massage your way down his belly, over his hips, and down his thighs. Avoid the genitals for as long as possible, building the anticipation. Whisper how big his penis is and how great it will look on film, and marvel at how hard it gets. When he can't take it anymore, begin massaging his testicles, shaft, and the head of his penis using the massage oil. Let him get hard, then back off and massage his thighs or belly again. Run your oiled hand all the way up his backside. Return to the penis to make it hard again, then move away and say, "We're ready for filming!" If you can, avoid bringing him to orgasm—save that for tomorrow's movie-making session!

Saturday

Are you ready for your big scene?

LIGHTS! CAMERA! ACTION!

It's time to make your own X-rated movie, an adventure that will surely heat things up—and create a keepsake, of sorts, for later viewing, reenactment, or revising! But before anyone starts stripping or moaning, set up and/or talk over these basics:

Equipment

Set up your camcorder (digital provides the best quality) and make sure you have enough memory and battery life for filming. If you're going to film the two of you, test out the tripod or other standing device for angle and position.

Lighting

Use ceiling-lit lamps to provide decent, low-impact lighting, and check the lighting by filming for a few seconds to see the results.

Perspective

"First-person" view is when you hold the camera and just film your partner (think Tommy Lee and Pam Anderson). This hides your face and focuses the attention on your lover. Be sure to use the "zoom in" and "zoom out" features to get close-ups or move back for the entire view. Alternatively, use the tripod and film the two of you together.

Rules

Agree on the rules—for example, not to share the video with your friends (unless you both agree beforehand), what to do with the video should you ever split up, and so on. Be sure to label the video appropriately and store it in a safe place once you get home.

Porn-Inspired Sex Moves

Time to turn on the camera and let the magic happen. Here are a couple of options to get you started.

LET HER BE THE STAR

You've agreed your female lover is going to be the star of this movie. Have some fun and make up a sexy title, such as *Gang Bang for Bonnie*, *Cathy Comes Alone*, or *Susie's Private Striptease*.

Decide on a script: Is she going to strip for the camera? Act out a secret desire or fantasy? Tell a story? Dress up appropriately.

Porn movies are usually sexier when the woman interacts with the camera. Talk about what you like sexually during the video, and open up a little bit and have some fun. Make sure to make eye contact with the camera—there is no greater turn-on than a sexy woman staring right into your eyes.

Try to have an orgasm on-screen, whether you accomplish that alone or with your partner's help. If you are at all nervous or embarrassed about being filmed, this could be more difficult than usual. Just take it slow and do your best to get comfortable.

If you're not sure where to start, try these moves and see where they lead:

- Say, "I want you to touch me" as you dip your chin and use your hands to lift up your hair. Slide your hands down your neck, across your chest, and down to cup your breasts, then gently squeeze your nipples as you arch your back.

- Say, "You make me hot" as you slide your hands down your belly, over your hips, and toward your thighs. Rub your mound with one hand as you squeeze your nipple with your other hand.

- Turn and walk away from the camera, then look back playfully and say, "Follow me." Once you're in the bedroom, move toward the bed, and start talking about a particular time you couldn't wait to get into bed with your lover. Act out the details and talk to the camera as you go through the motions.

- Alternatively, use the vibrator and pretend it's your lover that's turning you on. The Minx vibrator (pictured) makes a good costar: rub the shaft along your thigh, then slide it into your vagina, or let it pulsate against your clitoris and bring yourself to orgasm on film. Don't forget the sound effects! **(See below.)**

- For a different viewpoint, have him go down on you while you shoot the scene from above. The new perspective will add some variety to your film! **(See left.)**

TWO STARS, ONE MOVIE

Want to make a film of the two of you? Set up your equipment on a portable tripod, and check the angle to make sure all your action will be caught on film. Then try these moves for inspiration:

- Play with each other's nipples. Lick and then blow: the coolness will make nipples more erect and more sensitive. Don't neglect his nipples—sometimes he is even more into this kind of play than she is.

- Wet your fingers in your partner's mouth, then trail them down his or her chest.

- Lick your partner's ear and breathe into it softly. Ears can be as powerful a stimulator as the genitals, so whisper away.

- Stroke your lover's inner thighs slowly and lightly, then work up to longer strokes. Watch as your partner reacts. As you caress your partner's thighs, make tiny circles around the genitals with your tongue or a wet finger.

- Lick her labia in verrrry slow circles. Concentrate on the clitoris and increase intensity and speed as she nears climax.

- Lube up his penis with your mouth or lubricant and give him a hand job. Start with your thumb up and go up to the count of three, then down to the count of three. Wet the head of his penis with your tongue, then slide your palm over the top to switch to your thumb facing down.

- Tell him seductively that you want to go down on him. Slowly slide between his legs, maintaining eye contact. Use your lips and tongue to caress and tickle the head of his penis. Have him lay back, making sure the camera can capture his reactions! Use one hand to stroke his shaft and the other to cup his testicles. If he's game, lube up a finger and gently insert it into his anus. (See left.)

- Let the vibrator assume a supporting role: move into a semi-spoon position, but lean back so you can kiss deeply. Use one of his hands to stimulate your nipples while the second uses the vibrator to stimulate your clitoris. Lie back and let the camera capture the waves of pleasure undulating through your entire body!

pose for your centerfold

Love the camera? Here's another idea to play with this weekend: tell your lover you want her to play the budding centerfold, and you're the director of the photo shoot. As a virgin to the industry she must follow your every command.

Set up a sexy area for her photo shoot, such a fur-covered couch, a bed with silk sheets, or a bearskin rug in front of the fire. Ask her to dress in her sexiest lingerie or bikini, but to wear a short robe over her outfit. Load your camera with film (or charge your digital camera).

Have your lover pose for her centerfold shots, but tell her it's all about looking sensuous and sexy. You can direct her to remove her clothing, fondle herself, lean over suggestively, lie on her stomach and expose her buttocks, or pull her lingerie aside to expose her genitals. Take photos of each pose, then organize them into a slideshow and watch together.

Alternatively, have your lover do whatever turns you on—pinch her own nipples, finger herself, or wear handcuffs so you can insert a butt plug or dildo. Now's the time to pose her in the way you've always imagined, and capture it on film for future reference!

"Nor rural sights alone, but rural sounds,
Exhilarate the spirit, and restore
The tone of languid nature."
—William Cowper

Chapter 2:
DOWN ON THE FARM

Nothing beats the countryside for sensuous pleasure: the sweet

perfume of hay, the savory flavors of fresh fruit and honey, the feel of a soft blanket

as your lover lies with you in a pasture, sunlight streaming over your naked bodies.

Simply put, spending time in the country paves the way for romance, a little

down-home role-play, and some new positions for absolutely fabulous sex.

Planning Your Getaway

Check out these ideas and resources for planning your sexy farm adventure, and be sure to book your stay ahead of time.

- Many U.S. states, including Pennsylvania, Maine, Ohio, and Wisconsin, offer information regarding farm vacations. *Note:* Some farms are geared for families, so be sure to inquire about privacy or adults-only retreats. Do an Internet search for the state you're interested in, or check out www.pafarmstay.com, www.mainefarmvacation.com, or www.visitdairyland.com.

- Visit a dude ranch for a true cowboy adventure. The Dude Ranchers' Association website lets you search dude and guest ranches by state, adults only, spa activities, cabin accommodations, and more. Visit www.duderanch.org for more information. Canada also boasts a number of dude ranches: websites such as www.bcguestranches.com, which targets British Columbia, can provide more information.

- If you're looking for something exotic, consider renting a villa or farmhouse in Italy for the week (visit www.villa4vacation.com). If you want to stay stateside but want your own place, do an Internet search for "farmhouse vacation rentals" and you're sure to come up with plenty of ideas. Alternatively, try your local Craigslist site for vacation rentals, or visit one of the many "house swap" websites for opportunities to trade homes with someone in another state or country.

- Book a converted barn. Located on Puget Sound, just a ferry ride away from Seattle, is the Big Red Barn Getaway—a real barn built in the 1890s, then converted into a tiny inn. Visit www.bigredbarngetaway.com for more information.

Packing for Pleasure

In addition to your getaway clothes and toiletries, don't forget these sexy supplements to your suitcase for your sexplay and farm adventure:

- Role-playing outfits: cowboy boots, denim skirt, overalls, eyelet blouses, short cutoffs, jeans, gingham or denim shirts, halters, bikinis, boxers, or other country- or farm-inspired clothes

- Jeans and shirts that can get dirty

- Bandanas (for wearing or light bondage)

- Sex toys (dildo, vibrator, or other favorites)

- Spicy role-playing clothing: leather boots, leather vest, riding crop, leather chaps, cowboy boots, leather gloves, cowboy hat, hog-tying rope, and so on.

Friday

Nature is full of simple pleasures that allow you to connect (or reconnect) as lovers. Here's how to start out the weekend right.

NIGHTTIME FLIRTATION UNDER THE STARS

Once you arrive at your destination, grab a blanket, a couple of pillows, and a bottle of wine. Head out and set up a love nest under the stars, then try these activities:

- Try to find the Big Dipper or other constellations. Pick a star out of the sky and name it after your lover. Invent a constellation and tell a little love story of its mythology: be as silly or as sexy as you like. ("Now, this group of stars is called 'The Little Boner,' and for very good reason! You see, long ago . . .")

- Talk about your favorite outdoor sexual fantasy. Do you want to make love in the grass? To have sex deep in the woods on a carpet of moss? Fantasize and visualize together: What romantic things do you imagine doing outdoors? What might inspire you to try new things sexually—a new activity or location, or an activity we've done before?

- Find a secluded pond or lake and go skinny-dipping in the moonlight. There's nothing like swimming naked to make you feel free, fresh, and totally relaxed, and the nighttime atmosphere will make it feel romantic and mysterious. When you're done swimming, towel each other off and take turns brushing each other's hair, wrapping each other in a blanket, toga style, or cuddling together to get warm.

- Try this outdoor routine: start making out on the blanket, then indulge in some heavy petting. No sex, and no orgasms allowed—just plenty of groping, fondling, and heavy kissing.

Saturday

Every man fantasizes about a romp in the clover with the lonely farm girl or a quickie in the hay with the milkmaid, and here's your chance to act out that fantasy.

FARM FANTASIES

First things first: you'll need to scout out a private location for playing out your fantasy, such as a secluded meadow, an abandoned barn, or an empty shed.

Start by picking a role for both of you: ladies can play the innocent virgin farm girl who needs sex instruction, the naughty milkmaid who likes nooky in the hay, or the quiet, shy girl next door who's really a vixen at heart, while men can play the experienced farmhand, the farmer's shy and timid son, or the horny teenager next door who masturbates every night while watching the farmer's daughter undress.

If you're the innocent virgin farm girl, dress in overalls with a tiny top underneath, or put on your shortest denim cutoffs and tie a shirt up at your waist. Put your hair in pigtails and tie a bandana around your neck (this might come in handy later for light bondage!). Then tell your lover (the experienced farmhand) to pretend he's teaching you the ins and outs of sex. Ask him all kinds of questions: What type of kisses does he like best—slow and sensuous, or quick and flirtatious? Which does he prefer—deep French kissing or gentle tongue talk? How does he feel about you gently nipping his neck with your teeth, lightly scratching his back with your nails, or groping his hard-on through his pants? Let him command your every move, and try to pretend like you've never done this before—be timid and hesitant at first, and make him tell you what he likes best. (No matter how long you've been lovers, you're sure to learn something new!)

- Take his hand and place it over your heart, then slowly move it down to cover your breast.

- With your other hand, touch the side of his face, then take his other hand and move his fingers so they touch your lips.

- Kiss his fingertips and slowly lick them.

- Men, let your hand fall lower and lower, slowly making your way to her thighs, then move between them.

- Feel the heat between her legs, as you lightly push your hand against her, making small circular motions through her clothes.

Playing the naughty milkmaid and the farmer's shy and timid son? Dress the part of a milkmaid (think flowered dress and no undergarments) or the farm girl (short denim cutoffs, red checkered blouse or bikini top, or even a halter made from bandanas). This time it's your turn to lead him by the hand and show him all the details of the birds and the bees. Both of you are timid, but very curious; you are anxious and very eager to move forward. Remember, it's going to be just like your first time . . . well, your first time with a bit more knowledge.

- Kiss slowly, then stop. Kiss deep and passionately, then stop.

- Play with the idea of going further, but then be coy with each other, acting shy to take the next step.

- Unbutton her blouse; unzip his pants. Let your hands slowly touch these previously "unexplored" areas. Show restraint.

- Let your partner guide you in how to touch his or her most private parts.

- Direct each other with words like "slower," "faster," "deeper," and "harder" so you each learn how the other likes to be touched.

- Have him lie as still as possible while you kiss his lips, face, and neck, all the while stroking his arms, chest, and back with your hands. Slowwwwwly undress him one piece of clothing at a time, then shower his exposed body parts with kisses and caresses. Draw out this naughty foreplay as long as possible, then when you're hot and wet, command him to kiss your nipples, manhandle your breasts or buttocks, and caress your clitoris with his tongue.

Farm-Inspired Sex Positions

Looking for a more exciting romp in the hay? Try these positions:

Traditional Cowgirl: Have your partner lie on his back, then lick his thighs, suck his penis, and fondle his buttocks to get him hard. Use lubrication if needed, then straddle him, face to face, and insert his penis into you. Place your hands on his chest for support, and ask him to fondle your breasts or pinch your nipples while you rise up and down. Need deeper penetration? Have him kneel, sitting back on his legs. Slowly sit down on his lap, straddling him again and tucking your feet behind you and onto his knees. Put your arms around his neck for support and have him hold your back for better control. After you're done riding your bronco, let him taste his own secretions: slide upward so he can stimulate your clitoris with his mouth and tongue. Raise or lower your body, or rock forward and backward, to increase your pleasure!

spicy role play

Want to spice up your role playing?

- **LADIES:** Get out those leather boots, your sexiest leather vest, and carry a riding crop. You play the domineering horseback riding instructor while he plays sex slave.

- **MEN:** Put on your tightest jeans or leather chaps, cowboy boots, and leather gloves. Carry a long section of rope and make her your Indian princess or Colonial girl captive. Strip her down, hog tie her if needed, and tease her into seduction, have your way with her, or force her to give you head.

The Stallion: This time the man is in control. Stand together, with the man behind the woman, then have her bend over a chair, couch, table, or counter for balance and just the right curvature for maximum penetration. Don't just grasp her hips—play with her nipples, hold her hair, apply pressure at the base of her spine, and gently add pressure as you thrust into her. If she says "Too deep!," listen and ease up! **(See left.)**

Reverse Cowgirl: Have your lover lie on his back while you climb on top, but turn and face his feet. In this position, you control the pressure and speed, and it's easier for you to manually stimulate your clitoris. When your man is nearing orgasm, grab his toes—a slight tug gives him even more sensation because the nerves in his toes are connected to those in his genitals! **(See below.)**

Raunchy Rodeo: Start with you on top of him. Have him bend his legs so you can lean against them, giving you more leverage for pushing. Grab the backs of his thighs and hang on for the ride. Want it deeper? Position your legs over his shoulders, which will deepen the penetration (just what he craves!), then lean back, rub your own nipples, and either stimulate your clitoris yourself or ask your lover to reach over and stimulate you with *both* hands!

get down—and dirty

You're in the country, where dirt and mud are a fact of life. Get ready to play in the dirt just like kids, but add in some flirty fun! Be sure to dress down, meaning wear clothes that can get dirty, ripped, or even ruined! Then try these playful ideas:

- Find a small hill or grassy incline. Lie on top of your lover and roll down the hill together. You'll feel like little kids again, and laughter is good medicine for your relationship.

- **GUYS:** If a spring rain on the farm has left a muddy patch somewhere, surprise your lover and hoist her over your shoulder—then threaten to drop her in. If she seems game, go for it. Go ahead, get muddy! What's more important: good fun and making a romantic memory, or clean clothes?

- Seek out a muddy patch and mud wrestle—that's right, wrestle! Dress in clothes that can get ripped off so you both end up naked in the mud. Wrestling is one of those playful acts that brings you in close proximity to each other, but once you're naked don't expect it to stay playful for long—act like the farm animals you're near and do it doggie style in the dirt! Be sure to bring along some towels or blankets to cover up while you make a mad dash to the shower or the nearby pond!

"While we were on vacation, I thought, 'Why not? Let's have a threesome. We're on vacation, it's something I've always wanted to try, it will make the trip all the more memorable ... so we did it, and wow! Time of my life!"
—Keri, 32

Chapter 3:
THE FRENCH CONNECTION

French kissing, French ticklers, ménage à trois—lovers can

learn quite a bit from the French! This doesn't mean having to jet away to Paris,

mon cher—it means borrowing a page from the French playbook of flirting and

speaking to your partner in the language of love (in and out of the boudoir). This

weekend, see how spicing up your twosome is as simple as counting *un, deux,*

trois—as in ménage à trois.

Planning Your Getaway

Even if you can't travel to Paris, you can still find a taste of France elsewhere. Consider these locations, all of which offer a taste of French culture, history, and ambience. Be sure to book your hotel ahead of time.

- Visit the French Quarter in New Orleans (once called Nouvelle-Orléans), a city founded in 1718 by two French noblemen. Check out Creole townhouses with lush courtyards and intricate iron scrollwork. For more information, visit www.frenchquarter.com.

- Imagine a 400-year-old walled city in France, and you've got enchanting Québec City, a romantic Canadian getaway located about six hours north of Boston. For travel and accomodation ideas, visit www.quebecregion.com/e.

- Many experienced travelers feel that Washington, D.C., has many of the same architectural elements of Paris—wide boulevards, mansard roofs, low buildings, and classic façades. Stay in the heart of the city or visit the Nemacolin Woodlands Resort, a French renaissance–style château located just a few hours from D.C. in the Pennsylvania countryside.

- The city of St. Louis was first founded by a French fur trader named Pierre Laclede Liguest in 1763, and its name was chosen in honor of the Crusader King, Louis IX of France. For more information, visit www.explorestlouis.com/visitors/index.asp.

- Maine has a long history of French influence, dating back to Colonial days. Lewiston, Maine, features a diverse culture of French charm, including a growing arts community and the natural beauty of the Androscoggin River. To find a romantic B&B, visit www.bbonline.com/me/lewiston.html.

Packing for Pleasure

In addition to your getaway clothes and toiletries, don't forget to pack these sexy
necessities:

- English-to-French dictionary, preferably *Talk Dirty French* by Alexis Munier and
  Emmanuel Tichelli

- Dress clothes for Saturday night's ménage à trois hunt

- Sexy lingerie, silk boxers, and other luxurious undergarments

- Anything black—the favored color of the French

Friday

Tonight, get into a French mood. Here's one tried-and-true way!

MUSIC AND FILMS, FRENCH STYLE

Break out a glass of Champagne—what else?—and queue up some French music or a film set in France to start off your weekend.

French Music

- *La Vie en Rose: La Môme* (EMI Classics, 2007). The soundtrack to the Edith Piaf biopic, for which Marion Cotillard won the 2008 Oscar for best actress

- *Café de Paris: 1930–1941: 24 Accordion Classic* (Music Club Records, Import)

- *C'est L'Amour: Romantic French Classics* (RCA, 1996)

French-Inspired Films

- *Betty Blue* (1986). Wild, unpredictable, and often nude girl enters the life of a French house painter. Not the happiest of endings, but hey, it's European.

- *Amélie* (2001). Innocent Parisian girl with vivid imagination searches for love and enlivens the people around her. Charm and romance to spare.

- *Last Tango in Paris* (1972). Marlon Brando stars in this notorious psycho-sex drama about an older American widower who begins an affair with a beautiful young Parisian woman. Intense.

- *Chocolat* (2000). France, chocolate, love, passion, Johnny Depp. Enough said!

- *Jules et Jim* (1962). François Truffaut's classic about a turn-of-the-century love triangle. Artsy.

- *Henry and June* (1990). American writer Henry Miller (who, as one character puts it, "writes about fucking") meets diarist Anaïs Nin, who is taken with Miller's mysterious girlfriend, June. Sex, Paris, art, Uma Thurman. Complex.

- *An American in Paris* (1951). A classic tale of a down-and-out painter who can dance as well as Gene Kelly. It's all just a setup for a long and elaborate dream/dance sequence, but a fun ride all the same.

put the French back in flirting

In the American dating scene, flirting tends to be a signal that says, "Hey, I'm really interested in you." Americans tend to reserve flirting for bars, bedrooms, and "the right moment." In contrast, Europeans consider flirting a language that can and should be used anytime, anyplace, with anyone. To Europeans, flirting can be a way of relating to people; it's a social lubricant, if you will, not unlike small talk. Flirting makes life more pleasurable, and most important, it often isn't intended to lead anywhere: it's flirting for the sake of flirting.

The French recognize, and rightly so, that flirting is an art—not something you master by merely delivering a pickup line or getting a smoldering look in your eyes. So try these moves on your lover this weekend and see where things lead.

When it comes to flirting, the three most important parts of your body have nothing to do with the sexual act: your eyes, your smile, and your hands. Sexy eyes are happy eyes: narrow and widen your eyes to communicate to your partner. Smile at choice moments: if you smile all the time, your smile has no impact. Similarly, use your hands for effect, to place a touch on an arm or twirl your hair at the right moment.

When speaking, drop your voice an octave, and speak softly: this will naturally draw the listener closer to you, make him more attentive to what you're saying, and feel comforted by your lowered voice.

Never come on too strong. Men, especially, need to be told that less is more, and often, no words are preferable to even choice words.

ménage à trois

A French term that literally translates to a "household of three" or a "family of three." Call it what you like, but this actually refers to a sexual encounter between three people: two men and one woman, two women and one man, or three people of the same sex. Some slang expressions for this French tryst include club sandwich, double peptide, Oreo cookie, three decker, triple shag, or lucky Pierre.

- *Before Sunrise* (1995). French student Celine meets Jesse (Ethan Hawke), a young American traveling in Europe on a train, and . . . *ooh la la!*

- *The Ninth Gate* (1999). Literature and mystery lovers will enjoy Johnny Depp (again) in a quest for the devil's book. Lots of scenes in Paris, and Emmanuelle Seigner plays "The Girl."

Saturday

Time to get out there and see the sights. And to try for some new experiences.

MÉNAGE À TROIS

What's a Parisian paradise without letting your mind delve into the possibilities (and pleasurabilities) of having a ménage à trois, the best way to say threesome! Here's how to get three times the pleasure.

Verbalize

Talk to your lover about the different threesome possibilities. Would you prefer another woman or another man? What is your fantasy? What role does your lover want the third person to play—passive observer? Active participant? Something in between?

Dirty Dialogue: Dare to Go There
For Her
- Option #1: "I can imagine our threesome being with another man . . . the thought of two men wanting me, pleasuring just me, makes me wet just thinking about it."

- Option #2: "Being with another woman, feeling her soft curves, her even softer lips all over me, while you watch and join in on the fun . . . that puts me over the edge."

For Him

- Option #1: "I would feel like a voyeur, watching you being ravaged by another man . . . it will let me see your pleasure and learn more about what really gets you hot."
- Option #2: "It's one of my ultimate fantasies to watch you with another woman . . . there isn't anything much hotter than watching you explore and be explored by female flesh."

Take Action

Once you come to the decision on whether it will be another woman or another man, then it's time to find this lucky third wheel. Here are your options:

- Hit the town and size up the crowds at local restaurants and bars. Flirt. If you get any kind of response, take the chance and just come out and ask the person whether a threesome is something that piques his or her interest.

- Look in the local newspapers or websites that cater to people finding people with like interests. No strings. No problem.

Go for It

You've done it—you successfully picked up another person to join your sexual *soiree*. Now what? Be sure to establish the code word (see box at right), and practice safe sex all around.

- Skip the baby talk you usually do in bed. That would be a buzz kill for the third wheel.

- Tell your addition exactly what you want. Try only fooling around with the new person, or only make out with your partner while the new person watches and takes his/her pleasure into his/her own hands.

- If your threesome stars two guys and one girl, try having the newbie lie on the bed with the woman lying with her head on his chest but facing up. Then let her partner go down on her while the addition plays with her nipples. Perfect for those who aren't going to go all the way with this threesome.

- To go all the way with your third, you can be as daring as trying double penetration, or go for doggie-style sex while the other man gets a blow job.

"THE PROPOSITION THAT TWO'S COMPANY BUT THREE'S A RIOT."

—FRED MULLALLY, *THE PENTHOUSE SEXICON* (1968)

know the code word

Just like with S&M play, it's important to have a code word that you can say to your partner if you want to abort this threesome mission. If that word is said at any time during your dalliance, both of you should respect it and remove yourselves from the situation, or kindly tell your "guest" *merci*, but *au revoir*.

- If your threesome features two girls and one guy, go for a sixty-nine position with the two ladies and let the man work his way into the equation . . . he chooses which side to take. Alternatively, oral sex for all can be super stimulating. Situate yourselves in a circle and make the ultimate "O!"

"MY HUSBAND AND I HAD A THREESOME WHILE WE WERE ON VACATION AND I HAVE TO SAY, IT WAS THE BEST IDEA! ANONYMOUS, NO EXPECTATIONS, AND WE WOULD NEVER RUN INTO THAT PERSON AT OUR LOCAL SUPERMARKET."

—ILENE, 37

other options

If you are very interested in having a threesome but want to keep it as just that—an interest, not something to really act out—there are some great ways to almost take that threesome to fruition.

- Flirt up a storm with others at the bar, but know you are just going home with your partner. It gets the juices flowing and takes you close to what it would be like to be with another person without actually breaking that barrier.

- Meet another couple with the same interests, but who don't want to have sex with anyone else. You can all have sex in the same room, watch each other, and yet never really interact. (Local newspapers and websites can also help with this quest.)

- Make the third party be your favorite vibrator. Double the fun? Check. Double penetration? Check!

French-Inspired Sex Positions

Feeling adventurous? Try these positions for some variety this weekend!

Rond et Rond: This is "round and round" in French. Pull out your French tickler—a condom or penis ring with textural additions such as bumps and curves—and try sex with the man on top (and plenty of in and out action). Prop a pillow under her buttocks, then have her move round and round, which will focus all the pressure on her clitoris!

The French Open: With the man on top, open your legs wide and bend at the knees, resting the heels of your feet on his bottom. Pull him toward you with your legs as you also pull yourself up and press into him. Get ready for more stimulation—and all the control over when you orgasm! **(See below.)**

Racy Rendezvous: Sit on your partner's lap and gyrate to your heart's content. Have him kiss and nuzzle your neck and breasts, suck on your nipples, and grab your buttocks to pull you closer. Grind deep into each other—and don't forget the French kissing. (**See above.**)

The Encore: Ladies come first! Let his orgasm be the encore. Instead of having him come inside you, let him come on you. Ah, the money shot. Popular in porn, yes, but also super hot and dirty in the best way possible. Watch as he comes to see how his penis reacts to his tugs. There really isn't a hotter sight at that moment.

"WHAT'S MY TOP FANTASY? SEX ON A TRAIN FROM NICE TO PARIS! IT'S DOABLE. I'VE DONE IT. AND I WILL DO IT AGAIN."

—STEVEN, 27

"If you are having sex with someone who is not on the same frequency that you are on, it can be very problematic. The greatest karmic transfer occurs in having sex with someone."

—Dr. Frederick Lenz, Zen master

Chapter 4:
TANTRA FOR TWO

This weekend, tap into the ancient traditions of Tantra

for making your sex more focused, intense, and orgasmic. No, you don't need

hours and hours for finding pure bliss, but rather an open and ready mind for

exploring new territory, both inside and outside the bedroom!

Planning Your Getaway

You can practice Tantra-inspired sex at home just as easily as you can in an exotic location, but there's no doubt that your surroundings can help you move into a different state more easily and help you relax by getting away from your everyday routine or responsibilities. Try these ideas when planning your Tantra getaway.

- Book a hotel, a motel, or an inn that allows for the maximum privacy, the quietest of settings, or plenty of access to quiet and remote locations for truly unwinding, breathing deeply, and reconnecting with your lover. Visit www.selectregistry.com for ideas.

- Visit a destination designed for connecting mind, body, and spirit, or try a wellness retreat, such as the Omega Institute (www.eomega.org). Located in Rhinebeck, New York, Omega offers such sessions as "The Art of Sexual Ecstasy: A Gentle Introduction to SkyDancing Tantra" and "Sharing the Path," a couples retreat designed for greater intimacy, spiritual connection, and joy.

- Book a spiritual retreat at www.findthedivine.com or visit www.retreatsonline.com to book a silent getaway with your lover.

- Attend a Tantra workshop, retreat, or seminar using websites such as www.tantra-sex.com/tantra.html, www.blisstantra.com, or www.sacredloving.net.

- Try an adults-only or a romantic travel planner like www.adultsonlytravel.com, www.lovetripper.com/honeymoons/index.html, or www.excellent-romantic-vacations.com.

Packing for Pleasure

In addition to your getaway clothes and toiletries, don't forget these important extras:

- Yoga wear or light-fitting, comfortable clothing

- Sexy boy shorts for her

- Form-fitting boxer briefs for him

- Exotically scented massage oils

- Silk scarves (for playing and wearing)

- Eye makeup for enhancing your eyes

- Scented candles

- Feather

Friday

Time to get started on your weekend of togetherness by learning some more about Tantra.

INTRODUCTION TO TANTRA

Tantra is a Sanskrit word for an Eastern spiritual and sexual philosophy that emphasizes experiential approaches to life and lovemaking. The word *Tantra* can be translated a number of ways, including "weaving," "continuous process," "manifesting," "showing," and "expanding." Weaving together male (represented by the Hindu god Shiva) and female (represented by the Hindu goddess Shakti), Tantra unifies man and woman as lovers as well as the masculine and feminine qualities within each of us.

The primary lessons of Tantra are ones to incorporate into your everyday sex life:

- Live in the moment, or be "present" in your sexual encounters.

- Recognize the equality of the sexes and that each person has masculine and feminine energy.

- Extend the concept of consciousness from the mind into the body, thereby connecting the spiritual and the physical.

- Get inside your sexual experience and out of your head.

- Fully connect sexually to yourself and your partner.

- Discover your sexual energy and move it around your body to create desire, sustain arousal, and build orgasm.

THE RELAXING BREATH

One cornerstone of Tantra is breath control. Tonight, practice the relaxing breath together, which helps calm your nerves and bring new focus to your lover.

Start by sitting cross-legged on the bed. You may want to position yourselves facing each other, or sit side by side so that you can hold hands. All you have to do is close your eyes and breathe. You are easing into a meditative state, which will relax your body, aid digestion, and put you in the same peaceful place as your partner. Take a deep breath, in and out. Repeat.

- Listen to the rhythm of your breathing and recognize the uniqueness of your own breath.

breathing and orgasm

Breathing also has a lot to do with your intensity of orgasm. Keep these tips in mind while taking it all in.

- The faster you breathe, the more excited you will get.

- Breathe through your nose to de-stress, but breathe through your mouth for great sex.

- If you are having trouble reaching orgasm, pay attention to the way you breathe. Do you hold your breath? Try deep breathing instead. On the other hand, if you breathe very deeply and cannot come, try short, quick breaths instead.

- Coming close to orgasm? Try breathing from your diaphragm or core (yoga breathing) to help the orgasm build and make it more intense.

- Try breathing in tandem with your partner. Enjoy the feeling of the two of you breathing in the same rhythm, at the same time; it's like you're part of the same body, with the same energy.

- If the spirit moves you, say something heartfelt to your partner. Speak in a calm, soothing voice, and incorporate breathing and speaking so that one works with the other. Start with something simple, such as "I love you." Elaborate: "I appreciate how hard you work every day." Focus on a detail: "I like hearing the sound of your laughter." Or talk about a cherished memory, such as your wedding or when you first met. Keep it simple and short—you don't want to dominate the exercise.

Saturday

Today you'll explore each of the concepts of Tantra: sexual meditation, breath control, eye contact, kissing, touching, focusing sexual energy, and moving sexual energy. Get ready to experience your lover in new and fascinating ways!

TANTRA FOREPLAY

Sexual meditation and breath control can be thought of as Tantra foreplay. Once you master these two basic skills, you'll be ready for further Tantra exploration.

Sexual Meditation

What, you may ask, is sexual meditation? Simply put, it's meditation with an erotic focus. Like any form of meditation, follow these guidelines, but then take note of where your meditative experience takes a turn into the sensual zone.

1. Seek out a quiet or secluded spot, then sit or lie down in a comfortable position. Set the scene by dimming the lights, lighting candles, or putting on soft background music. Make sure there are no interruptions, such as cell phones or people coming to the door, and that outside noise is kept to a minimum.

2. Remember, there's no judgment or expectations; be open to what happens or doesn't happen. Breathe deeply and slowly, relax, and clear your head by letting go of the chatter in your mind. The goal is to quiet the mind and body so that sexual energy can speak and come forward.

3. Picture an erotic image—a penis, a flower, a breast, or whatever stimulates your erotic senses. Keep your focus on the image and continue breathing in a pattern of long, slow, deep breaths. Relax. See where your erotic image and your breathing take you.

Breath Control

Breath control is an essential—but easy to learn—skill that can help relax and focus your sexual energy, sustain arousal, and intensify orgasm.

1. Sit or lie down in a comfortable position. The goal is to breathe in a circle, which can be as small or as big as you want. At first, keep the circle very tight: circulate the breath through your nose, mouth, throat, heart, and lungs. Once you feel comfortable, expand the circle and let the breath circulate additionally through your belly and genitals. Feel your breathing as a continuous, smooth circle.

BUILDING THE CONNECTION

Eye Contact

In Tantra, the eyes are seen as the gateway to the soul. Strive to make love with your eyes open, maintain eye contact with your lover even when one of you is having an orgasm, and use your eyes to speak your own special language. This can help deepen your connection and build intimacy. Just as closed eyes are associated with shyness, open eyes are truly baring your soul!

Kissing

If the eyes are the gateway to the soul, the mouth begins the journey. Kiss whenever and wherever you can. Kiss deeply, kiss passionately, or try this simple exercise: while kissing, deliberately inhale your partner's exhalation and exhale your inhalation into his or her mouth. This will bring you even more in sync.

Touching

Erotic touch is part of good lovemaking, but in Tantra sex, touching is not enough—you must *become* the touch. In real terms that means getting the pressure just right. When the touch is just right, the feeling is of flesh melting together. Pay close attention to your lover's response and you can learn when the pressure is too much, too little, or just right.

FOCUSING AND MOVING SEXUAL ENERGY

Tantra is based on the belief that energy flows through the body's energy centers (also known as chakras), from the genitals through the spine, stomach, throat, forehead, and finally to the top of the head. Energy flow is as critical to Tantra sex as blood flow is to life.

Before you can move sexual energy around, however, you have to feel it. Start by imagining a small fiery ball of sexual energy just below your navel. Breathe deeply and slowly, and imagine that little spot of energy flowing and growing.

Next, use your breath to move that energy down to your genitals. Now imagine a fiery coil of sexual energy located at the base of your spine. Uncoil it and move it into your genitals. Do you feel the tingling sensation? You have now moved your body's energy into your genitals!

SEXUAL EXPLORATION

Now that you're well on your way to mastering the basics of Tantra, you can use these tips to experience yourself and your lover in new ways.

Take the time to explore each other. Light the aromatic candles you brought along and get the scented massage oils and silk scarf ready. By the soft, flickering light, slowly take off each other's clothes, all the while gazing into each other's eyes and intermingling kisses. As you reveal the shoulder of your partner, take a moment to kiss it; when you unzip and remove your lover's pants, softly lick your partner's thigh.

"I LOVE BLINDFOLDS! YOU CAN BE HAVING PLAIN OLD MISSIONARY-STYLE SEX, BUT ONCE A BLINDFOLD IS IN THE MIX, THE KINK FACTOR TAKES THE WHOLE EXPERIENCE UP A NOTCH."

—JENNIFER, 30

When you are both totally naked, lie down side by side on the bed and take a moment to really look at the beauty of your partner. See how her hips curve into her sides; gaze at his shoulders rounding up to his neck. Admire what makes her a woman and him a man. Whoever is doing the massaging first gets to wear the silk scarf as a blindfold. Warm the massage oil in your hands, then slowly rub your sweetheart's body. It's going to be a new experience because without the sense of sight, everything else is heightened.

Tell your partner what you feel:

- "Your shoulders are so strong, I love to feel them move."

- "My favorite part of your body is your thighs; they are so smooth, and when we make love they feel so good against my body."

- "Your neck feels so elegant and sexy."

- "Your hands deserve a lot of attention. They always know how to touch me in all the right places."

Then share the way it feels when you touch your partner:

- Describe the amount of heat you feel coming off your partner's body.

- Talk about the smoothness of your lover's skin.

- Have you partner give you the feather and gently trail it down your lover's back.

- Let the partner being massaged explain the reaction of his/her skin when you tickle it.

- Ask your partner where he or she enjoys the feather play most.

Tantra-Inspired Sex Moves

You've connected on new levels and now you're ready to connect deeper and enjoy the benefits of your newfound intimacy.

- After you've both had an orgasm, let your fingers do the walking to your partner's hot zones. Softly massage his balls or slowly rub her clitoris in small circles, then help each other work your way to ecstasy one more time. Bliss is beautiful!

- Try the Downward Dog yoga position. The increased blood flow to the woman's head will actually increase her sensitivity.

- Experiment with standing positions where one of the woman's legs is draped over her partner's shoulder.

- Go longer.

- Try the Deepest Connection position. Ladies, sit on top of your man, face-to-face with your legs around him. Let his erect penis inside you, but don't gyrate. Just be. Try slowly straightening out your legs and let your hands explore one another. **(See below.)**

- While you are still physically connected, drip some wax slowly down your own chest and then your partner's. Feel the penis become more erect; the vagina walls will tighten. Ladies, slowly gyrate your hips in small circles while deeply pressing into your partner. Rub your clitoris against his body, slowly, slower . . . hold it there. You will be amazed at the buildup of tension you already have. You will feel so close to coming, but teeter there, hold out, let that tension build. **(See above.)**

- Do it in the dark, or wearing a blindfold. You've become so in tune with your own bodies, the darkness won't hinder you; instead, it will inspire you. **(See right.)**

- Make love missionary style and synchronize your breathing.

- Ladies, move your legs from around his body to over each of his shoulders. This position is great for G-spot stimulation, and with both of your hot spots truly at the hottest they can be right now, you will probably feel a bit heady with excitement. Take yourselves almost to the point of no return, then slow down. This sexual marathon gives you the power to control the intensity of the orgasm. The longer you hold out, the bigger the reward. When you've reached that peak, release all the energy you have built up in your climax.

EYE-OPENING SEX

Here's a new twist on open-eye sex: masturbate in front of a mirror while your lover is out, in the shower, or otherwise occupied. As you come, make deep, intense eye contact with yourself. Loving yourself with open eyes will boost your confidence— and don't be shy about sharing your entire experience with your lover.

- Lie on the bed with a view of the mirror (if possible) and watch yourself in action.

- Close your eyes and envision your partner going down on you.

- Touch other parts of your body with your free hand.

- Relive past sex moments you had with your partner.

- Don't be afraid to moan when nearing orgasm. You're going to reveal your activity when your lover returns. Oh yes . . . in detail!

- When your partner comes back, spill the beans on your dirty deed: just come out and say, "I just masturbated," with a big smile on your face.

- Fess up to the naughty details.

- Take your partner's hand and show him/her how you touched yourself.

- Tell your partner about what it was like when you masturbated, such as "I imagined it was your finger inside of me. And when I came, it was like I felt you coming inside me, too," or "I closed my eyes and thought of your mouth on me. It was hot and wet, and felt just like when you touch me."

"Stolen kisses are always sweetest."
—Leigh Hunt, English poet and essayist

Chapter 5:
SECRET GETAWAY TO MOTEL 69

If you've ever known someone who had an affair—or you

yourself have imagined having an affair—then you may know the steamy, addictive

feelings of passion and secrecy that go along with cheating. Don't get me wrong:

this weekend adventure isn't about infidelity, but it is about tapping into those

feelings of stolen kisses, secret longings, and clandestine encounters to ignite

a spark of passion with your lover!

Planning Your Getaway

You're looking for the perfect roadside rendezvous: the charming but often ignored roadside motel that caters to one-hour, one-day, or one-night encounters for secret lovers. Your destination needn't be seedy or downtrodden, but rather the kind of place that you'd usually drive right by—that is, unless you were looking for a hidden spot for nooky on the sly! You may not need a reservation, but call ahead to guarantee availability.

- Find a classic, roadside motel that you can visit by car. Plan a road trip using a site such as www.roadtripamerica.com.

- Get in your car, drive toward a town you've always wanted to visit, and find a motel along the way. This works well in the off-season for resort or tourist areas, or in locations that don't get much traffic. Better yet, book a motel in your own town or the next town over and you won't have to travel far at all!

- Like a little history thrown in? Consider a motel along Route 66, the infamous highway that goes from Chicago to Los Angeles. And keep the words of the famous song *Route 66*, by Bobby Troup, in mind.

- Visit a town or city that's well known for 1950s-style or "Doo-Wop" hotels, such as Treasure Island or Key West. Visit http://treasureislandflorida.org/motels.htm or www.keywest.com/hotel.html for more information.

Packing for Pleasure

In addition to your getaway clothes and toiletries, don't forget to pack these sexy and sly elements. This weekend is all about easy access, so pack with that in mind!

- Easy-access clothing, such as button-down shirts, short skirts, low-cut blouses, and so forth.

- Loose boxers and thong panties (easy off and easy maneuvering)

- Sunglasses, hat, wig, and other items for disguise

- Massage oil

- Road map

Friday

Where do secret lovers meet? Wherever they can—in a car, at a little-known restaurant, at any location that's off the beaten track! Tonight, pick a location for your clandestine meeting and really play up the "hidden" nature of your romance.

- **In the Car:** Find a darkened parking lot or an abandoned road for hot and steamy foreplay. Remember, you can't keep your hands off each other, but you're not allowed to orgasm—save that for your Motel 69. Instead, indulge in some heavy petting.

- Experiment with different types of kissing—try some light and airy kisses alternating with deep, penetrating lip-locks. Expose your lover's breasts or penis, and play to your heart's delight using your hands, lips, or mouth—but don't let her or him get fully undressed or come. Intermingle deep French kissing with lower lip nibbling, hand roaming, body thrusting, and dry humping—it's the perfect way to foreshadow things to come!

- **In the Restaurant:** Wear a disguise so no one will recognize you: dark glasses, hat, wig, or unusual clothing (but don't make it too memorable!). Make a game of it—hold hands or play footsie under the table, but pretend you're just "friends" or "business colleagues" when the waitstaff comes by. Sneak into a dark corner, a stall in the men's bathroom, or the coat closet for some hot, stolen kisses and quick, urgent groping—but don't get caught!

"HER KISSES LEFT SOMETHING TO BE DESIRED . . . THE REST OF HER."

—AUTHOR UNKNOWN

Saturday

The signs on the highway are letting you know that lodging is at the next exit, and neither of you can wait. Remember, this weekend is a special treat—you don't normally get your lover all to yourself, completely alone. Get ready for checking in and checking each other out—and savoring every inch!

When you sign in with the hotel clerk, act like a couple getting a room for the first time together. Kiss your partner on the cheek and pinch his/her butt when getting your key. On the way to the room, take a moment to kiss passionately in the elevator. Who cares if there are others around? Once in the room, don't bother to unpack . . . just undress. Use only the light from the bathroom to illuminate the room. Get out the massage oil and take off all your clothes.

Time to lube up, ladies, and get ready for a full-body rubdown. Men, here is your guide to getting her revved and ready.

- Pour massage oil in your hands and rub them together to warm the oil.

- Start from the small of her back, working your hands up toward her shoulders, applying light pressure and slowly building intensity.

- Alternate sitting beside her and on her bottom.

- Lean yourself into her—the feel of your flesh on hers is going to turn both of you on.

- Ask what feels good—with all the revealing conversation that has taken place between the two of you, now is not the time to stop.

- Work your way down her legs all the way to her feet and up again.

- Linger longer, everywhere. This massage is going to make her anticipate every touch—where are your hands exploring next? From the tips of her toes to running your hands though her hair, then down her arms to her fingertips—not one inch of skin will be left with a yearning to be massaged.

- Let your mind run wild. Envision yourself inside her as you massage. Pay attention to how her body responds.

- Talk as your hands roam, remember the touches she liked best, and repeat those moves when you make love. It's a great way to learn exactly how she reacts to certain stimulation.

- Ladies, do not hold back. Moan when it feels good, and who cares if the front desk clerk calls with a noise complaint! Let go, express yourselves—this is all about the two of you as a couple. Direct his hands where it feels best, and feel all your stresses from the past week just melt away in his touch.

- Once her backside has been fully explored, it's time for her to turn over and share in the rubdown.

- Add massage oil to your hands, rub them together, and while sitting on the bed facing each other, rub each other's chest, shoulders, and arms.

- Bring your bodies together—the woman's legs on each side of her partner's, in a face-to-face straddle.

- Bring your chests together, arms in an embrace, and feel how slippery your skin is against each other.

- Men, hoist her up, holding her bottom, and direct your penis into her.

- Ladies, do you want clitoral stimulation? You know you do! This position is great for more sensation where you love it most. With your body upright, you can further push him into you and when properly lubed, the clit gets a lot of action. Never be afraid to use your hands—your own or your partner's; the extra action will provide an explosive orgasm.

Steamy Sex Moves from Route 66

Need some other ideas for increasing your passion? Try these moves:

Palming: You know those dual-action vibrators that simultaneously stimulate your vagina and your clitoris? Your lover's hand can do the trick as well. It's perfect for self-love or for your partner to please you. With the man sitting behind or lying beside you, have him insert a finger (or two) into your vagina and then let his palm lie flat on your outer labia. Have him press his palm against your clitoral area and gently move in small circles.

Driving Stick: It may not be the first technique that comes to mind, but never forget the appeal of a good old-fashioned hand job . . . provided there is a lot of lube, of course.

- Using both hands and lots of lubrication, move your hands up his penis as if you were climbing up a rope, hand over hand; then do the reverse, and climb down, hand over hand.

- Take his erect penis firmly with one hand, and with the other hand, make a fist and gently massage his perineum (the area beneath his testicular sac). Make clockwise and counterclockwise motions with your fist.

- With one hand, massage his testicles; with the other, rotate his erect penis around in a circular motion, like the moving hand of a clock.

- Don't be shy about asking your man how he masturbates. Tell him, "I want to get you off the way you like it, baby." Encourage him to instruct you on just the right motion and just the right speed. Ask him if he will come faster with you speaking or you staying silent, and oblige him. (It'll be your turn soon!)

- Talk to your man as you're massaging him. Flatter him by telling him what a big cock he has; squeal with happiness when he comes, saying, "That's my man!" or "Atta boy!"

Under the Hood: Show him the wonders of your clitoral hood!

- Let your lover masturbate you, armed with lubricant and a dildo or vibrator, if you please. Give him the option of getting you off by hand, or by mouth, or both. Guide him to apply the right pressure, in the right motion, over your clitoral glans.

- Talk to him (without getting clinical) about how a clitoral orgasm happens and what it can feel like. Your lover needs to be told to start slow, become steady, hit the right frequency, and keep it going. Tell him to give your clitoris slight, gentle licks with his tongue. Encourage him to use his fingers to gently, slowly, massage your labia and explore.

- If your lover is dying to penetrate you with his hand, tell him to position his hand so that his thumb is applying pressure to your clitoris, and his finger is gently exploring you vaginally. If you're game for more than one finger, tell him to add one at a time until you reach your happy limit.

"STOLEN KISSES REQUIRE AN ACCOMPLICE."

—GLADIOLA MONTANA AND TEXAS BIX BENDER, *JUST ONE FOOL THING AFTER ANOTHER: A COWFOLKS' GUIDE TO ROMANCE*

"The first time my husband and I tried chocolate body paint, we laughed and laughed. The second time, our sexual attraction was ravenous! The foreplay of laughter was a big part of it ... and the chocolate licking, of course."

—Nicole, 28

Chapter 6:

APPETITE FOR LOVE

This weekend getaway, centered on the sensuous pleasures of food, will leave you satiated in more ways than one. You'll never look at food (or your lover!) the same way again, and you'll go home with plenty of delicious tips and memories.

Planning Your Getaway

There are many ways to indulge your passion for food and sex this weekend, including selecting a location that's known for great food, planning a culinary vacation or getaway, visiting pick-your-own farms for harvesting your own favorite foods, or checking out a local food fest or celebration. Be sure to book your hotel ahead of time.

- Plan a culinary vacation or gourmet getaway, or attend cooking classes or demonstrations at locations throughout the United States.
Visit www.epitourean.com.

- Book a culinary vacation in the Napa Valley of California, a region known for its winery tours, gourmet food, and romantic inns. If you want to learn to cook or train side by side with a chef, visit websites such as www.winecountrygetaways.com or www.gourmetretreats.com.

- Search the Internet for inns offering culinary-themed weekends that can include cooking instruction, food and wine tastings, or a gourmet meal with food and wine pairings.

- Locate a food, wine, chocolate, or other gourmet food festival, trade show, or exposition, and book a hotel for that weekend. Search the Internet for events serving up your favorite foods. The options are endless: chocolate lovers weekend, chowder fest, or chili cook-offs, to name a few.

Packing for Pleasure

In addition to your getaway clothes and toiletries, don't forget these sexy treats. This weekend is all about the sensual pleasure of food, so keep that in mind as you pack edible panties, chocolate treats, and finger foods!

- Erotic edibles, such as candy panties, chocolate body paint, etc.

- Erotic fruit and sundae fixings: strawberries, raspberries, or peaches; chocolate and/or caramel sauce, whipped cream, maraschino cherries, firm bananas, sprinkles, and so on.

- Clothes for play as well as dress up for a romantic dinner out (or in)

- A silky scarf that can be used as a blindfold

- A big appetite—for sex *and* food!

Friday

Plan for a sensuous dinner, upon arriving at your destination, that includes age-old aphrodisiacs and foods with serious sex appeal. Be sure to order more than one item off this list of "naughty nosh":

- Avocados—This fruit's tree earned the name "testicle tree" from the Aztecs because it grows in pairs.

- Basil—This herb is said to promote circulation (essential for long-lasting hard-ons!).

- Caviar—Rich in zinc, this delicacy increases the flow of testosterone.

- Celery—This vegetable contains androsterone, a male hormone that may cause your female lover to snuggle closer!

- Chile peppers—The physical reactions to eating hot chile peppers mimic those of sex, such as increased heart rate and sweating. Who knows? Maybe your brain thinks its time for some nooky!

improving your own secret scent

You've heard the saying "You are what you eat." You also smell like what you eat. For anyone who's overdosed on garlic, you know it lingers on your breath and your skin for days, and everyone knows how eating asparagus can affect the smell of your urine—and your semen! But the reverse is also true: if you want to smell sweeter, eat more sweet foods, such as honey, fruit, sweet potatoes, and carrots. Here's a little-known fact: what you eat specifically affects the scent of your genitals and the smell and taste of a man's sperm.

- Chocolate—Due to the presence of phenylethylamine and serotonin, which are both "feel good" brain chemicals, chocolate mimics that feeling of falling in love, and when you already are, it makes it all the more intense.

- Cucumbers—Phallic yes, but the scent is said to increase the blood flow to your female lover's genitals.

- Honey—In ancient Persia, newly married couples drank a honey mixture every day for a month to increase their sexual desire. Over time this led to the term *honeymoon*.

- Mustard—This spicy condiment is said to push sexual glands into overdrive.

- Oysters—Can you think of any other food that more closely resembles the female genitals? They are also high in zinc, which is associated with boosting male sexual potency.

- Papaya—This fruit is said to mimic the female hormone estrogen, which can increase your female lover's libido.

PLAY WITH YOUR FOOD

Take a cue from your kids and play with your food. However, make this adult version of food fun as naughty and messy as you dare.

- Ladies, lick the shaft of a cucumber or stalk of celery while looking into your man's eyes. Show him what's in store for later.

- Have fun feeling an avocado before you cut into it. The skin is firm, but the flesh underneath is tender. Feel your partner's breasts to compare.

- Slowly peel back the skin of a banana and gently show your partner how far you can put it into your mouth.

- Berries, particularly raspberries and strawberries, please the palate. Along with peaches and cherries, they will leave a sweet scent on your breath and can be erotic if you feed them to each other.

- There's something about chocolate that forces you to say "mmm" when you eat it. Let a little chocolate sauce drip from a wooden spoon onto your partner's waiting tongue.

- Sticky, gooey, sweet—yes, we're talking about honey. Drizzle some on each other and feel the sensation as your bodies rub together.

- The mere act of eating oysters is sexy. Stare into each other's eyes as you slowly suck the meat from the shell.

Saturday

Today's theme is enjoying both food and your lover, at the same time. Here's the idea: let your lover build his own sundae using *you* as the dish. The menu includes mountains of luscious whipped cream; gooey chocolate syrup; creamy caramel sauce; sweet maraschino cherries; firm, peeled bananas—and, of course, *you!*

Start by hand feeding him cherries and letting him lick chocolate off your fingers. Then undress in a slow and seductive manner and position yourself provocatively on a towel or sheet. Try any of the following ideas or come up with your own:

- Dip your nipples in chocolate sauce and have him lick or suck the coating off.

- Outline your breasts in whipped cream, then have him remove the topping with wet, sloppy kisses.

- Create a caramel trail from your neck to your inner thighs, and have him follow it with his tongue.

- Hide a cherry in your genitals or belly button and ask him to find it.

- Hold a cherry in your mouth and pass it back and forth as you kiss deeply.

- Cover your clitoris or his penis with whipped cream, then lick it off.

- Masturbate with the banana (either rubbing your clitoris or inserting it partially into your vagina while he watches), then have him eat the remains, take over the work with his tongue, or use his penis to continue the action.

- Blindfold your lover and have him or her stay close by. Choose three places on your body to pour a few drops or a nickel-size puddle of chocolate syrup, then tell him or her to find the sweet treasure using only the tongue.

- Dribble chocolate syrup on or around your clitoris, spoon whipped cream onto your labia, and top it all with tiny sprinkles. Tell him, "Eat me!"

great movies with food and romance

- *9½ Weeks* (1986). One of the main items on the menu in this '80s-era soft porn feature film is the kitchen scene in which Mickey Rourke's character feeds a blindfolded Kim Basinger a series of sensuous delights. Watch, learn, and give it a try yourself.

- *Like Water for Chocolate* (1992). A young Mexican woman channels her passion into her cooking, with mystical (and sensual) results. Love! Sex! A naked woman on horseback! *Olé!*

- *Last Tango in Paris* (1972). In this gritty and notorious film, Marlon Brando introduces Maria Schneider to anal sex by means of a stick of butter.

- *Flashdance* (1983). Few women have eaten restaurant lobster as erotically as Jennifer Beals in this '80s classic. And as if her oral play weren't enough, she takes time to massage her boyfriend's groin under the table with her bare foot. What a feeling!

- *Malèna* (2000). As if this movie weren't enough of a lust-a-thon, Monica Bellucci squeezes fresh lemon over her naked torso and enviably perfect breasts. (*Note:* Get the unedited European version, not the sanitized American release.)

- Decorate his backside with chocolate syrup, whipped cream, and sprinkles, then eat it all off while licking from his anus all the way around to the tip of his penis.

- Paint your lover's body with the chocolate body paint and lick it off. Spend extra time flicking your tongue over his or her nipples and really draw out the pleasure of this intimate body worship.

- Dress your female lover in the edible panties and enjoy eating every last bit off of her.

screaming for ice cream

- **ONE SCOOP.** Both of you eat some ice cream, making your mouths very cold. Then kiss each other on the mouth, the neck, the arms, the nipples, all the while with that cold feeling on your lips and tongue.

- **TWO SCOOPS.** Give your partner some oral sex using your favorite flavor of ice cream. Either go down with some ice cream in your mouth or lick the ice cream off your lover's body.

- **THREE SCOOPS.** Being penetrated or penetrating when cold ice cream is added to the equation has all the benefits of oral sex, only this time you both can feel the hot/cold sensations at the same time. If you really want to go wild, light a candle and balance the cold with some drips of hot wax.

Culinary Adventures in the Bedroom

You're done devouring your dessert—now get ready to lavish some pleasure on your female lover.

- Place one finger in your mouth to get it wet, then watch the look on her face as you slowly move your finger inside her and continue your licking there.

- As you pull your finger out, lightly suck on her clitoris.

- Slowly move your finger in again, this time deeper, and increase the speed of your licks according to how her body reacts.

- Wet a finger on your other hand and, as you move the first back into her vagina, move the other slowly into her anus, as you lick her clitoris in a heavy stroke.

- Keep both fingers insider her, wiggling slowly and softly, as you alternate between lightly sucking on her clit and licking her all over, exhaling your hot breath onto her to enhance the sensation.

- Try an "mmm" sound with your mouth as your lips reach her clit. The vibration will melt her.

His penis, perfectly protruding, is just waiting for your lips to take the pleasure to the next level—orgasm.

- With your hand firmly grasping the base of your partner's penis, and with a very wet mouth, concentrate on the head.

- Slowly and rhythmically squeeze the base as your mouth hums lightly around the tip.

- Wet his entire shaft with your tongue, licking from top to bottom, strengthening the tip of your tongue as you trail it down the center of the underside of his penis. (There are lots of nerve endings there!)

- Take his member deep into your mouth—as far as you can go to meet your hand still firm on his base. Then move your mouth and hand up his shaft in one movement.

- Remember, the key here is lots of wetness!

- Let your hand slide up over his head, then down again, but this time put his member between your pointer and middle fingers for an extra-tight grip.

- As you continue these movements, let your other hand gently play with his balls.

- Be daring and lube up one finger and gently insert it into his anus, tickling his prostate, while gearing up for the ultimate finale—adding his own gooey sauce to your menu!

"MY HUSBAND NEVER WAS EXPERIMENTAL IN BED, YET HE WAS SO ADVENTUROUS WHEN IT CAME TO ANYTHING CULINARY—HE *IS* A CHEF. ONCE I OPENED UP AND TRIED NEW THINGS IN THE KITCHEN, HE REALLY OPENED UP AND WANTED TO HAVE SEX WHENEVER I OFFERED TO HELP HIM COOK! I LEARNED HOW IMPORTANT IT IS TO SHARE EACH OTHER'S PASSIONS."

—KARINA, 40

peppermint tingler

Really want to blow your lover's mind when you give him a blow job? Buy your favorite flavor of Altoid mints, then chew some of the mints before sucking on his penis. The tingling sensation you feel in your mouth when you chew these mints will intensify the sensations for your lover!

"There is a bit of insanity in dancing that does everybody
a great deal of good."
—Edwin Denby, American poet and dance critic

Chapter 7:

TWO TO TANGO

Dance can be flirtation, intimacy, or foreplay set to music.

When you and your lover move together, hip to hip and breast to chest, you're

engaging in a mating ritual as old as seduction itself. Perform a sultry shimmy,

back bend, or hip roll for your lover and you're using dance as foreplay at its most

powerful and passionate. This weekend, use dance to create fun, flirtatious, and

orgasmic sex play that you'll never forget!

Planning Your Getaway

Need help planning your dance-theme getaway? Try these ideas as a starting point.

- Visit a dance "destination." Companies such as www.stardustdance.com post weekend getaways to a resort or spa offering dance workshops, night and day dancing, DJs, and so forth.

- Conduct an Internet search for hotels, resorts, or inns that cater to dancing couples—these package deals offer a variety of '50s, big band, or Sintra-style dance bands for patrons.

- Ask a travel agent about specialty or vacation packages to locations such as Argentina, which includes tango dance lessons and a city tour of Buenos Aires.

- Check out www.dancevacations.com for dance workshops, festivals, and competitions across the nation—and beyond.

- Book a dance cruise. Many ocean cruise packages include dance instruction in everything from ballroom dancing and tango to hip-hop, salsa, and swing.

- Pick a destination or two, then do an Internet or Yellow Pages search for dance studios offering lessons. Websites such as www.studioofdance.com and http://dancedirectoryplus.com let you search for dance studios by location. Make sure you book a lesson (and hotel room) beforehand!

Packing for Pleasure

In addition to your getaway clothes and toiletries, don't forget to bring these necessities for your sexplay and dance lesson:

- Sexy music with a hot beat for Friday night (CD player and CDs, portable stereo, docking station and iPod, etc.)

- Slow and sensual music and candles (optional) for Saturday night lap dance

- At least one new (unseen) set of sexy lingerie (including bra, panties or G-string, garter, and stockings), high heels, blouse and skirt or dress (to strip out of) for lap dance

- Body glitter and/or body paint for lap dance (optional)

- Low-cut dancing dress or sexy blouse and skirt (with dancing shoes to match) for tango dance lesson. Tango is a sexy dance, so dress appropriately: plunging necklines, form-fitting fabrics, and barely there mini skirts will all look great!

- Suit or handsome dance outfit for his tango dance lesson

- Sex toys, lubrication, condoms, or other sexy accessories

Friday

Once you've arrived at your destination, dress up and go out to dinner, or just head out for a drink or two. When you get back to your hotel room, put on some music. It doesn't matter what kind of music, as long as it has a sensuous beat.

Start to dance. Hold each other tight, and press against each other. Rub your hands over his buttocks, kiss her neck, and caress his shoulders. Keep dancing while you massage his penis under his pants or pinch her nipples through her dress. French kiss, but keep dancing. Slip off his jacket, and undo his tie. Unbutton his shirt. Unzip her dress, and pull it down to her waist. Nuzzle her breasts, stroke his chest. Lick her cleavage. Play with his nipples. Keep moving together, grinding your crotch areas together as things heat up. Unbuckle his belt. Let her dress fall to the floor. Unzip his pants and let them fall to the floor. Place your hands on each other's buttocks. Slide your thighs in and out. Keep grinding, dancing, and gyrating. Slip your hand inside his boxers. Stroke his penis to the music. Slip your fingers into her panties and flutter her

movies with the right moves

Need a little inspiration to find your groove? Rent one of these movies for viewing before or during your dance getaway:

- *Save the Last Dance* (2001). A young aspiring ballerina falls for a hip-hop dancer. If they can dance together, you and your lover will look like pros!

- *Swing Time* (1936). Fred Astaire and Ginger Rogers: his gentlemanly elegance and her earthy sex appeal made dance history.

- *Dirty Dancing* (1987). The perfect prelude to a little dirty dancing of your own.

clitoris to the music. When you're hot enough to climax, dance over to the nearest support—wall, post, table, whatever. Pull down his boxers, pull down her panties, and have sex standing up. You just danced yourself naked—and learned a new position!

Saturday

Daylight has arrived, and it's time to spend a full and glorious day focused on dancing with your lover. Start your day with a scrumptious brunch, then head out for your private tango lesson.

LEARN TO TANGO

Without a doubt, the tango is one of the world's sexiest dances. Born in the bars and brothels of Argentina, this form of ballroom dancing has been described as joyful, romantic, fiery, spicy, sensual, and loving—all characteristics you can find on the dance floor *and* bring to your sexplay.

For the man who loves the chase—and the woman who loves to have him catch her—this passionate Argentinean dance features chest-to-chest moves and a continued close embrace. The tango isn't just a dance—it's a metaphor for sexual pursuit. Starting with a nod from your lover, signifying his desire to dance with you, the dance continues in a series of moves resembling stylized foreplay.

visit a strip club

If the sight of half-naked women turns you on as much as it does your man, then try visiting an upscale strip club together. The key is to let the pulsating music, barely clothed dancers, and steamy atmosphere heat you both up—then take your passion back to the hotel room where you can let loose. Let the wild, sexy atmosphere bring out your adventurous side, and remember that your lover may be turned on by more than just the dancers; your confidence, watching you interact with other women, or just the novelty of it all will heat him up.

While you're at the club, watch the moves the dancers use (and take mental notes for later). Ask your lover which dancer he likes best and why. If you're feeling really comfortable, pay for that dancer to give him a private lap dance, or to give the two of you a private couple's dance.

And here's a bonus from strip club insiders: women in the audience at strip clubs often get a lot of attention from the dancers—if you're dressed nicely and looking hot you could even end up on stage with a stripper! Talk about the ultimate turn-on for your lover!

Once you arrive at your lesson, soak in all the details of this sensuous dance, and even flirt with the instructor if it turns you (or your lover on).

Keep these tango basics in mind as you take your lesson:

- Simply put, the tango is basically an ornamented, stylized walk that moves around the room. The dominant movements have a stalking feel to them, with highly articulated movements, much like a stalking cat. Other times the movements are sharp, like a quick foot flick.

- There is more than one rhythm in tango, but the basic one is slow, slow, quick. This means you pick up and place your feet onto the floor in a slow move, followed by a slow move, and then a quick step.

There are several ways the dance moves can carry you right back to your hotel room! Try these moves:

- **Reverse Rhythm:** Another rhythm is quick, quick, sloooooowwwwww. To use that rhythm to your advantage, try lying on the bed with your hips close to the edge and have your lover kneel on the floor. Ask him to penetrate you quickly, quickly, and then slowly draw his penis almost all the way out of you. Repeat the action as needed until you can't control the rhythm!

- **Rhythm Reinvented:** Transform the basic tango rhythm of slow, slow, quick into sexplay actions, such as soft, soft, hard; gentle, gentle, rough; lick, lick, nip; or shallow, shallow, deep. When stimulating your lover's clitoris, for example, use a soft, feathery touch, repeat, then zero in quickly for a direct stimulation. This tease, tease, touch! rhythm can be used to draw out the pleasure as long as needed to bring your lover to orgasm.

- **Movement:** Sometimes the movements of the tango are slithery, other times staccato. Try a slow and slithery version of seducing your lover: start at his toes and act like a snake, licking your way up his body, rubbing your breasts along his thighs, your clitoris on his knee, and your hands slowly up his backside. Or let him seduce you with sharp and rapid-fire movements, adding in a little rough play with your nipples and breasts while he penetrates you quick and hard from behind.

"DANCING IS A PERPENDICULAR EXPRESSION OF A HORIZONTAL DESIRE."

—GEORGE BERNARD SHAW, IRISH PLAYWRIGHT

Dance-Inspired Sex Moves

As you know, dancing can be incredibly seductive. So go back to your hotel room and put your dance moves to work in the bedroom! Be prepared for an orgasmic reaction.

Start by putting on some slow and sexy music and dimming the lights or lighting some candles to create a sensual scene. After you've set the mood practicing your new dance moves, have your lover sit in a chair without sides, either naked or in just his underwear. Alternatively, have him stay fully dressed and tell him the house rules: he cannot touch you (but you can touch him).

Go into the bathroom and change into your sexiest outfit: bra and G-string, garters, stockings, high heels, and a short sexy dress or blouse and skirt to cover up your lingerie. Make sure all your clothes can be easily removed, and the heels make your legs look long and inviting. Free free to get creative with body paint and/or glitter!

Then follow this lap dance routine, or use these professional lap dance and striptease moves to create your own personal show:

- Keep all your movements very slow and sensual, and maintain eye contact at all times. Never let your hands or fingers hang loose—if you're not sure where to put them, rub them up and down your body, along your arms, or through your hair.

- As you walk toward your lover, sweep your feet on the floor, lower your chin and smile seductively, and sway your hips slightly.

- Lift up your hair from behind using both hands and dip your chin down, then give him a sultry, penetrating look. Gyrate your hips slowly.

- Touch your arms, stroke your neck, run your hands over your body, and touch your hair frequently. If you have long hair, flip it up and back a few times during your dance.

- Roll your hips. Move your hips back and forth sideways, or try the advanced version: bend your knees, then roll your hips in a circular motion, leaning over to expose your cleavage. Run your hands down your thighs, then back up, and push your breasts outward. Strip off your dress or blouse, then slowly remove your skirt, keeping every movement slow and sensual.

- Squat and stroke. Keeping your belly tight, slowly bend your knees downward, sliding your hands down your legs to your knees, then back up to your crotch. Massage your pubic area suggestively or lick a finger and dip it into the front of your panties.

- As you stand up from the squat, pivot around and bend over with straight legs. Push your bottom out, toward your lover, place your hands on your hips, and run your hands under your panties as if you're going to remove them, but don't. Push one hand through your legs and run a finger along your crevice, from your anus to your vagina.

- Stand up, circle back so you're facing your lover, and move toward the chair. Straddle the chair with one leg and lean inward, then push your breasts into his face, shimmy and gyrate close to his crotch, touch his hair, and pull his face toward you for a French kiss or cleavage rub.

- Back off, then move in again and lift one leg onto his shoulder, exposing your crotch at eye level. Rub your hands all the way down your body, then pull aside your panties to touch yourself ever so briefly. Take your leg down and slowly pivot so you're facing away from him, then slide your bra straps off your shoulders, unhook your bra, and turn back toward him. Push your arms together to create cleavage, then slowly peel off your bra and toss it in his lap. Play with your breasts, squeeze your nipples, and rub your hands down your belly, over your crotch, and around to your bottom.

- Move back toward the chair and shimmy as close to him as possible; put your hands on his shoulders and pull his face toward your breasts, but keep moving slowly and sensually from side to side. Stand up, slip off one shoe, then put a leg on the chair and slowly roll off your stocking. Repeat with the other leg, then slowly roll the garter off your hips and toss it on his lap.

- Stand up, turn around, bend over, and let him enjoy the view. Then hook your fingers on your panties. Slowly pull them off, giving him a slow and drawn out look at your backside, then get down on your hands and knees and crawl away, swinging your hips slowly from side to side. Turn and crawl back toward his feet, then slowly slither your way up his body, brushing your breasts, belly, and crotch against his legs, knees, and body until you're sitting in his lap. Kiss him deeply, rub his bare penis, or through his underwear, and let things take their own course!

"I SEE DANCE BEING USED AS COMMUNICATION BETWEEN BODY AND SOUL, TO EXPRESS WHAT IS TOO DEEP TO FIND FOR WORDS."

—RUTH ST. DENIS, EARLY MODERN DANCE PIONEER

"Climb the mountains and get their good tidings. Nature's peace will flow into you as sunshine flows into trees. The winds will blow their own freshness into you, and the storms their energy, while cares will drop off like autumn leaves."

—Leigh Hunt, English poet and essayist

Chapter 8:
INTO THE WILD

Being one with nature is a great way to become one with each other. Just imagine the erotic activities you and your partner can explore, whether it's learning how to be a "naughty Boy Scout," zippering up for sleeping bag sex, or experiencing the ultimate back-to-nature sensuality: outdoor sex!

Planning Your Getaway

There are as many ways to plan a nature-oriented getaway as there are natural places to explore. Use these ideas as a starting point for planning your weekend adventure, or research national parks, nature preserves, or beaches that are accessible by car.

- Plan a camping trip using sites such as www.koa.com/where, www.gocampingamerica.com, www.reserveamerica.com, or www.recreation.gov.

- Plan an "adventure travel getaway" using a website such as http://gorptravel.away.com.

- Go to www.nudistparks.net for a map of nudist parks, campgrounds, resorts, "non-landed clubs" (nudist gatherings that are organized at a rented pool or a person's backyard or home), and even nudist timeshares.

- Stay in a tree house! The Cedar Creek Treehouse is a private mountain retreat in the woods of Washington's Mount Rainier, located 50 feet up in a 200-year-old western red cedar tree. Visit www.cedarcreektreehouse.com for more information.

- Book a B&B, an inn, or a motel in an area close to a park, forest, nature preserve, beach, or lake. Visit www.bnbfinder.com or www.bbonline.com.

- Plan a visit to a national park, such as Yosemite National Park, which offers beautiful meadows, 100-foot-tall waterfalls, and majestic mountains for hiking and exploring. For general information visit www.nps.gov/yose, and for lodging in and around the park visit www.nationalparkreservations.com.

- Find a vacation rental in a remote location. The Moosehead Lake region in Maine, for example, is just 40 miles from the Canadian border and offers thousands of acres filled with wildlife and natural beauty. Visit www.mooseheadlake.org or www.mooseheadrentals.com for more information.

- Michigan is home to more than 11,000 inland lakes, and the Upper Peninsula region is 90 percent forest. Visit www.rentalbug.com to find a cottage rental.

Packing for Pleasure

In addition to your getaway clothes and toiletries, don't forget to pack these supplies in your backpack for outdoor sexplay:

- If you're going camping, be sure to bring along a tent, lanterns, flashlights, batteries, sleeping bag, air mattress, portable stove, blankets, food, and rugged clothing.

- For any outdoor excursion, don't forget bug repellent, sunscreen, blankets, beach towels, solid hiking boots or footwear, and layers of warm clothing for sudden rain, drops in temperature, or change in elevation.

- Pack picnic foods, finger foods, wine, rose petals, massage oil, and sex toys as desired.

Friday

Pack up your gear, head out to nature, and pitch your tent!

PICNIC BY FIRELIGHT

Build a fire in your cabin or light a campfire outdoors, then spread a blanket on the floor or the ground. Dress yourself in sexy lingerie, perhaps with a flannel shirt or jean shirt over. Ask him to wear silk boxers under a flannel shirt or outdoorsy outfit.

Open your favorite champagne or wine. Lay out an extravagant feast that you can eat with your fingers, such as chocolate kisses, olives, or melon wrapped in prosciutto. For a special treat, serve caviar on a bed of crushed ice, with a small spoon to ladle it onto pieces of toast. Serve decadent chocolate truffles or juicy berries dipped in whipped cream for dessert. Feed each other the foods, and be sure to savor every bite before moving on to the next. If you spill anything, lick up your mess.

After you've had enough of tasting the food, taste each other. Disrobe each other slowly. Slide your tongue over your lover's skin. Taste his lips, his neck, and his nipples. When you kiss, prolong the exploration of each other's mouths. Relish the taste and aroma of all his body parts. Have your lover fill his mouth with champagne and trickle the bubbles over your nipples or clitoris; before you perform fellatio, take a sip of bubbly and wrap your mouth around his penis for an amazing sensation.

To spice things up, use finger foods to stimulate and tease your partner. Rub a tiny pickle against her clitoris, then lick off the juices. Ladle caviar around his penis and eat it off, or make a bikini bottom from caviar and ask him to go down!

TELL GHOST STORIES

As the darkness comes, cozy up together on the blanket, either under the stars or in the warmth of your cabin. It's ghost story time!

Bring along a book of scary stories by such authors as Stephen King, Edgar Allan Poe, H. P. Lovecraft, or Anne Rice, and start reading to each other with extra emphasis on scary words.

Go for those classics that you told when you were a kid, such as "The Man with the Golden Arm." If you or your partner went to camp as a kid, you're sure to remember a few.

Recall any personal experience you may have thought you had with a ghost.

As you share these tales, you'll feel your body respond with chills, and you'll feel more alert (a defense mechanism). With every breeze, you'll think you hear someone creeping up on you, and you may even believe you see shadows beyond your campfire. All this will turn your body on, and bring you into the arms of your partner.

"MY BOYFRIEND AND I NEVER CONSIDERED OURSELVES 'OUTDOORSY' BEFORE, BUT ONCE WE TRIED IT—RENTING A CABIN IN THE WOODS AND GOING ON HIKES —WE INSTANTLY GOT HOOKED. AND FINDING A NEW INTEREST FOR THE BOTH OF US TO SHARE REALLY INJECTED SOME NEW ENERGY INTO OUR RELATIONSHIP. AND INTO OUR LOVE LIFE, TOO! WE STARTED FEELING SO ATHLETIC, SO IN TOUCH WITH NATURE'S BEAUTY, OUT THERE HIKING. AS SOON AS WE CAME HOME, WE STARTED PLANNING OUR NEXT TRIP TOGETHER!"

—NORINE, 23

Saturday

Whether you're hiking, walking, or trailblazing in the woods, any outdoor adventure opens up the possibility for *l'amour en plein air*, as the French say. Outdoor sex under a blazing sun or beneath the gentle caress of a summer breeze has a sensual feel like no other.

Before your begin undressing and getting it on, however, keep these tips in mind:

- **Rule #1:** Ensure your secret spot is secluded. Otherwise, you'll have some explaining to do to the park ranger, and you may even risk arrest for indecency.

- **Rule #2:** Dress for the occasion. Both sexes should skip the underwear, and zippers and snaps are better than hard-to-manage buttons. Ladies, go for items that open in the front, and gents, go slow when you're zipping back up.

- **Last but not least:** condoms are not biodegradable. Respect nature, and pick up after yourself.

TAKE IT OUTDOORS!

There are many scenarios for making love outdoors, including a hidden lake or pond (go skinny-dipping first!), a secluded meadow full of flowers, or a bed of moss in a dark and mysterious forest. Use these ideas as a jumping-off point, or find your own favorite natural spot and heat up the great outdoors!

Pond or Lakeshore Loving

Who among us hasn't imagined a sexy interlude on the grass next to our favorite skinny-dipping spot? Spread out a blanket and drape the towels close by (that is, unless you want to air- or sun-dry your naked bodies).

Start out by coating yourselves liberally with sunscreen and having a fun outdoor wrestling match. If your lover is taller or heavier than you, then make it fair by tying one arm behind his back or binding his feet together. The object of the game? To wrestle each other naked!

Once you're undressed, take a dip in the lake or pond and snuggle close to each other in the water. There's nothing as sexy as the feel of skin underwater, and the buoyancy can help you wrap your legs around his waist or slide up against him from the back. Come out of the water, lie down on your blanket, and indulge in the classic 69 position. Let the sensation of the elements, such as the feel of a soft breeze, the warmth of the sun, or even the smell of dirt arouse and further ignite your primal passion!

outdoor role-playing

Use some of these ideas for more games that are sure to heighten your pleasure!

- **MOUNTAIN MAN:** The woman is a bookish biologist hiking deep into the woods to collect specimens of plants and flora (hair in a bun, eyeglasses pushed up on her nose). An unexpected discovery of boot prints leads her to a remote log cabin, nestled in the forest. There, a rugged survivalist lives: a man of few words with arms conditioned by log cutting and heavy lifting. An invitation indoors for fresh water and food by a crackling fire stirs a long-buried passion in our timid biologist, and before you can say "Grizzly Adams," the biologist's hair is down, her clothes are off, and she is bent over a woodpile, receiving the Mountain Man's thrusting power. Go ahead and cry out: there's no one for miles to hear!

- **LOVE OF THE LOST:** The man and woman are college kids, getting back to nature on a raft expedition in the Grand Canyon. When the sun turns hot, the man strips to his skivvies, and the woman leans over the raft to splash some cool mountain water onto her chest. Suddenly the waters bend into rapids, and our young rafters find themselves tossed and thrown, their raft punctured and their backpacks barely rescued as they swim furiously to shore. What to do! Soon night will fall, and the temperature will plummet. Doing what is necessary, they strip to their skin, put out their clothes to dry, and the man sets about trying to build a fire. The sight of her naked male companion crouching over a developing fire awakens something in the woman: thoughts of cave people, men and women who operate on instinct and appetite for survival. Night falls, and a bonfire sends embers floating up to the stars. The lovers huddle for warmth, and their bodies respond. Without warning, this innocent outdoors trip between classmates has become something more . . . !

- **NAKED SURPRISE:** The woman is a power executive who is engaged to be married, and her female colleagues pitched in to give her a private present: a weekend room for one at a "clothing optional" resort in the Southwest. The executive laughed, but she does, after all, need a vacation from work as well as from her wedding plans, and the option to go bare in the sun will erase those strap tan lines for her off-the-shoulder wedding dress.

Once at the resort, the executive finds that nudism becomes her: all those lunch breaks in the company gym have paid off. One afternoon, however, as she lays herself out for a naked sunbath and a heavy lotioning with coconut oil, she looks up and her heart goes from first gear to fourth: a man in a tight-fitting bathing suit is approaching her, and once her eyes go from his yummy form to his face, she realizes she knows him! It's one of the younger men on her staff, and here she is, naked as the day she was born (but more oiled up)! He smiles down at her, and says, "Fancy meeting you here," never revealing that the ladies in the office bought an extra ticket for the stud they knew their boss has always had her eye on. The executive stammers, trying in vain to cover her aroused breasts and cross her legs . . . but it's just her and her young colleague, and everything's out in the open (or soon to be, from the looks of the bulge in the young man's bathing suit). Suddenly those wedding plans seem a thousand miles away!

- **NAUGHTY BOY SCOUT:** Boy Scouts are supposed to know all the rules to surviving in the wilderness, and they are mentally and physically strong. Follow these rules to act out this classic game: Be Courteous. Let her come first. Oral sex is a great way to earn this badge! Be Kind. While going down on her, don't neglect the rest of her body. Pull her hands into your hair, circle your fingers around her nipples, and place your hands under her tush while squeezing it upward into you. Be Obedient. Have her ask, so you both can truly receive! As she gets closer to orgasm, ask her how she wants you to make love to her. Get dirty with your language if you know she likes it. Ask her if she wants some action from the glow-in-the-dark vibrator, then let her (and the light) guide you. This will put her over the edge. Be Helpful. Once she comes, her body will be reeling in pleasure, so when you move your penis into her, go slowly—her pleasure spots may be tight or ticklish. But you may also be able to get her to have a second coming. Try putting one finger in her anus or move one finger over her clit as you move in and out, around and around. Make this two times her fun.

In the Meadow

Seek out a meadow filled with flowers and lay down a blanket, or create your own "bed of flowers" in a private spot outdoors by spreading out a blanket and then covering it with rose petals.

Disrobe your lover in a sensuous way, then have him or her lie down naked on the bed of flowers. Brush the blossoms or petals all over his or her body. Gently caress the base of the throat with the softest petals, then use the blossoms to trace a path from the throat to the nipples, belly, shoulders, buttocks, or thighs. Create a ritual-like setting and adorn your lover's body with blossoms and petals. Tell him you're a bee looking for nectar and he must lie perfectly still while you eat, suck, or nibble the petals and honey away. Hide the petals or blossoms in your crevices and ask your lover to eat his way out of the garden.

Among the Trees

Start by playing a game of hide-and-seek around the campsite. Whenever you find your lover, remove a piece of his or her clothing. The winner (whoever stays dressed the longest) gets to tie the other lover to a tree (facing forward or backward) and force him or her to submit to your every directive. Try teasing her by tracing a small twig up her thighs or dipping a smooth stone in massage oil and running it over her buttocks. Or take it up a notch and spank him using a switch made from a branch.

Strip down as far as you please, but put your boots back on! Your lover will find a visual thrill in seeing your sensual shape juxtaposed with rugged footwear: plus, when you spread your legs or bend over to hug that tree, your feet won't slip during crucial moments.

When you make love in the woods, leave human language behind: communicate only with animal-like grunts, groans, trills, yips, and yelps. Not only will this bring out the animal spirit in you, but you may also enjoy the challenge of communicating with your partner in a new way!

Camping-Inspired Sex Positions

It's time to zipper yourselves up and face the challenge of . . . sleeping bag sex!
Some people think that to have good sex, there has to be lots of flailing about:
totally not true. Here are some great positions perfect for getting it on while zipped
in, or just to try for variety at the nearby-the-wilderness bed and breakfast:

- Try sex with your female lover on top, but put her legs between yours, with all
  legs stretched out straight. This allows for shallow sex and stimulates the opening
  of her vagina, which can be as sensitive as the clitoris.

- Have your male lover on top, and you entwine your legs in his. Use your legs to help him push into you, a maneuver that really turns him on and makes your vaginal walls tighten.

- Lie down side by side, facing each other, then use slow and deep penetrating movements. Use your hands to roam, grope, and pull you closer together. **(See above.)**

Oral sex is about much more than just one person being aroused. You both can satisfy your sexual hunger and also expand the meaning of sex.

- Before diving in, face each other and try massaging his head (the one attached to his neck!) or shoulders while he explores your breasts and hips.

- The 69 position is popular for a reason. But don't get so involved in your own performance that you don't reap the rewards of what is being done to you. Take turns with intensity so you both can really feel the pleasure.

- Try a side-by-side 69 so you both have a great angle. **(See below.)**

- While direct contact is extremely satisfying, it's not just your privates that can get turned on. If you want to take a moment to really enjoy what your partner is doing, nibbling your partner's fingers or toes will keep the action going.

"I remember my first kiss with my now-husband. We were lying on a beach blanket. As we were lying there talking, our hands touched. The next thing I knew I felt the salt of his sweat on my lips. I'll never forget it."

—Carlyn, 38

Chapter 9:
REALLY WET SEX

Water is naturally sensuous, so planning a weekend getaway that combines water, skimpy clothing, and sex could be the ultimate experience in hedonism. Beaches and beach towns are a natural draw, but if the beach is too far, don't forget the cool water of local lakes and ponds, water theme parks, or locations that cater to boating adventures—all of them offer potential for a sensual getaway and some *really* wet sex!

Planning Your Getaway

There are as many ways to plan a water-oriented getaway as there are lakes and beaches. Use these ideas as a starting point for planning your weekend adventure, or research lakes, watery resorts, exotic island destinations, or beaches you find appealing.

- Seek out water. Whether you're looking to rent a houseboat, visit a famous river or lake, or just rent a cottage on a freshwater lake, websites such as watergetaways.com offer plenty of ideas.

- Stay in a lighthouse. The Browns Point Lighthouse in Tacoma, Washington, lets you be the lighthouse keeper! Visit www.pointsnortheast.org for more information.

- Start out in a boat—the options are plentiful! Rent a canoe or kayak, plan a motorboat excursion, go waterskiing, take a sailboat ride, or book a white water rafting trip. Boats offer a fun and exciting form of transportation for your weekend getaway. Visit www.usobe.com for more information, or rent a houseboat using sites such as www.goplayoutdoors.com/houseboats_menu.htm.

- Visit an island. It could be as far as Hawaii, as exotic as Atlantis Paradise Island in the Bahamas, or as close as your local lake, but all islands share one thing in common: they're surrounded by water. Contact a local travel agent or check the Internet for travel specials.

- Look for unusual water-related activities, such as beach camping, visiting a natural hot spring, or booking a night in an underwater hotel. Websites such as www.soak.net let you search for hot springs by state; www.reserveamerica.com can help you find camping locations near or on the beach; and underwater hotels include Jules' Undersea Lodge in Florida (www.jul.com) and the Utter Inn in Sweden (www.privateislandsonline.com/utter-inn.htm).

Packing for Pleasure

In addition to your getaway clothes and toiletries, don't forget that the hot summer sun or the potential for swimming means only one thing when it comes to clothing— less is more:

- Cool, lightweight clothing, footwear, and sleepwear

- Mini dresses and sandals for her

- Cool linen shorts and tops for him

- Baby oil or sunscreen

- New bathing suits for him; bikini or tankini for her

- Waterproof lubricant, vibrator, or other sex toys

Friday

Tonight, head out to the beach, the pool, or the hot tub for some nighttime water play. Remember to bring along a flashlight, beach towels, and a blanket for snuggling!

FOREPLAY IN THE SAND

Sculpt each other's naked bodies out of sand, using your own body as a model, or make sexy sand prints by lying down and molding the sand to the contours of your body. Use your shovel to dig out a hole for sitting, then ask your lover to sit in the hole while you climb onto his lap.

Pretend you are Aphrodite, goddess of love, beauty, and sexual pleasure. (The story goes that she was born when Cronus castrated his father, Uranus, and threw his genitals into the ocean!) Adorn yourself in scallop shells and a necklace of seaweed. Ask your lover to lie on the beach, then crawl or emerge out of the ocean like a mermaid come alive. Worship his body by kissing him all over, teasing his inner thighs with your seaweed, and presenting him with the ultimate gift: a wet and sandy blow job with the waves crashing in the background.

POOLSIDE PUSSY

Tell your lover you have a nighttime poolside rendezvous planned, no bathing suit needed. All you need is private and secluded access to a swimming pool and a clear, star-filled night for this naughty nocturnal game.

Try this erotic version of Marco Polo: blindfold your lover and hop into the pool. Tell her she must find you based on your moans of pleasure (loud for close, soft for far). Once she finds you, reward your lover with a wet and watery kiss, an underwater groping session, or a quick finger in the vagina or anus. Then switch roles. Feeling really bold? Try making out on top of an inner tube, air mattress, or other floating pool toy.

HOT TIMES IN THE HOT TUB

There's nothing like soaking in a hot tub to wash away your worries, and everyone knows that a worry-free mind is open for naughty adventures. Just take care in the hot tub not to slip or submerge your head under water. Bathing suits are also optional here.

Ask your lover to sit on the bench, facing into the tub. Kneel on the bench, with your legs straddling him, then lower yourself onto his lap. Hold on to the edge of the tub for better support as you grind against him, using the water to help buoy you up.

Lower yourself onto your lover but face away from him, which will let him gently twist your nipples, stroke your clitoris, or massage your buttocks as you move up and down.

For some exotic foreplay, kneel in front of a water jet so it stimulates your clitoris, then ask your lover to enter you from behind for double the fun! Alternatively, have him sit or kneel in front of the water jet so it stimulates his anus. Kiss him passionately while you given him an underwater hand job.

Saturday

Are you ready for some really hot and wet sex? Then find a secluded spot and get off using one of these water-themed ideas, tips, or techniques.

A BOAT OUTING FOR TWO

Take the boat out into the middle of the lake (where you should have more privacy than anchoring near shore), enjoy a picnic, and go for a swim. Once you're back in the boat, offer to help him dry off. As you rub him down, rub your body up against him suggestively, then gently strip off his bathing suit while stroking his buttocks, penis, and legs. Ease him onto one of the seats, then start kissing him from the neck down. Give him a luscious blow job in time with the gentle lapping of the waves.

role-play: pool boy and horny housewife

Every woman loves imagining the fantasy of the hot, seductive pool boy who stopped by while she's sunbathing, so here's a role-playing game that anyone can indulge in.

Wear your sexiest bikini and your most seductive sandals. If you don't have a pool, create a make-believe poolside setting: drape a beach towel over your couch, serve some sexy summertime drinks, and get out the suntan lotion. Ask your lover to wear a summery shirt, shorts (or bathing suit), and flip-flops. Don't forget the sunglasses!

You're the horny housewife who wants to get tan—all over. The problem is, you can't reach your back to apply the lotion, so you need his help. Lie on your stomach, untie your bikini top, and ask him to put suntan lotion on your back. As he rubs you down, begin your seduction: moan suggestively, arch your back, push your buttocks against him, or dangle your arm and rub his ankle suggestively. Turn over suddenly, accidentally losing your top and exposing your breasts. Pretend to be surprised, but then tell him you like to sunbathe topless, and you'll need lotion on your front side as well!

Alternatively, set yourself up as if you were sunbathing topless, but you're getting hornier and hornier as you watch him clean the pool (or move around the room). Start to touch yourself, then just lie back and start masturbating—but command him to keep cleaning the pool. See how long you can prevent him from joining in the fun in the sun!

the pros—and cons—of suntan lotion

While feeling the silky smooth of suntan oil all over your bodies is super hot, be careful not to get the sunscreen in your privates. It can disrupt the woman's vaginal flora, which is no fun. Certain sunscreens and baby oil also break down condoms, so take care when mixing sunbathing and sexual pleasure.

ROW, ROW, ROW YOUR BOAT

Row or paddle a rowboat, kayak, or canoe to a deserted island or beach. Go for a swim, have a bite to eat, then tell your lover you want to play water nymph. Have him lie naked in shallow water, then swim out a short distance, turn around, and approach him from under the water. Try to touch, kiss, and stroke his feet, legs, and genitals as much as possible while under the water, then finally work your way up to giving him a blow job or climbing astride!

BUOYANCY IS BEST

In a pool or in the ocean, take advantage of her buoyancy in water to lift your lover, then carry, cradle, and embrace her. With your bodies submersed in water, the feel of the waves already rocking you back and forth, it's hard not to think about going at it right there. The buoyancy also makes it easy to try variations of positions that have proved difficult in the past. Ladies, wrap your legs around your man's torso, slip that tankini or bikini bottom aside, and float on.

BRING OUT THE ICE CUBES

Using an ice cube to stir and stimulate? Very sexy. Take an ice cube and run it slowly along his back. Spell some racy words and see whether he can tell you what they are. Trace the cube over your breasts, then pop it in your mouth, suck on it, and slip the ice cube into his mouth. Make ice cubes with fruit juice, and run them over your lover's body, licking the trail as you go.

the more the merrier, the wetter the better!

Renting a beach house with close friends is a good way to cut down on vacation expenses. There is a love life advantage, too, to planning your getaway this way: sexual experimentation can be easier when you're in the company of people you know and trust.

If you've ever fantasized about having sex in front of other people, who better to keep your secrets than your buddies? A roaring campfire, a bottle of wine, a late-night skinny-dip, and some friendly encouragement, and who knows what could happen! Moreover, being in a house that is not your own creates a neutral territory where "what happens here, stays here."

The key is that everyone in the house is on the same page. Talk with your partner and confer with your friends as to what is within bounds and most definitely off-limits. (It may be easier to be specific on the latter instead of the former.) And if what you're up for is a big thrill—say, partner swap—plan to try it closer to the end of the vacation than at the beginning, just in case something goes awry and someone wants to go home early.

Naughtiness needn't go that far, of course. Suggest some more innocent activities, such as nude coed sunbathing (and group lotioning), telling racy stories around the campfire, strip poker or other games, or truth or dare.

Waterfront-Inspired Sex Techniques

Get wet with these poolside-friendly positions.

EXPLORE THE SHALLOW END

The shallow end of the pool is where people linger when they don't want to go all the way in. Translate that to sex and you've got shallow penetration, which is often the most pleasurable for women. The first two inches of the vagina is known as the "orgasmic platform," and this is where most of your lover's sexual pleasure is derived (along with the 8,000 nerve endings that are in the clitoris—twice as many as the penis!). This is where the saying "It's not the size of the ship, it's the motion in the ocean" comes into play!

Get into a spoon position and keep your bodies relatively straight. The penis will enter in just a few inches, and his hands are free to wrap around and stimulate those sensitive spots. Alternate between oh-so-slow movements and fast action to see which pace suits you best. Sometimes a slow start, fast middle, and super slow finale is the best way to spend your time in the shallow end.

DIVE INTO THE DEEP END

If you want to get completely wet in a pool, you dive right into the deep end. When it comes to sex, if you want it all and you want it now, deep penetration is the answer. Men are big fans of deep penetration, and for good reason—it stimulates the entire shaft, and even the testicles get in on the action when they hit the base of their partner's ass. If the penetration is slow and deep, and your lover moves in close and tight, he can also stimulate your clitoris. Many women also enjoy taking in every inch of the penis—it's a feeling of intense intimacy.

What are the best positions for deep penetration? Reverse Cowgirl (see page 31) works great, and it's also good for G-spot stimulation. You can also try missionary, but experiment with the woman's legs up and apart as the man kneels with a straight torso. The higher the woman's legs, the deeper her lover can penetrate. **(See left.)**

FIND A LOUNGE CHAIR

If you want some quick and hot sex, then lie face down on the beach lounger, and arch your ass in the air as he enters you from behind, his feet firmly planted in the sand. Men, lightly pull on your lover's hair, and the combination of the arching and penetration will make everything feel tighter—meaning orgasms come faster. **(See above.)**

"I do all my best work in bed."
—Mae West

Chapter 10:
BOOTY-LICIOUS BED-IN

Spend the day in bed? It's a relaxing and sensual weekend activity that

will reconnect you with your lover in many new and unusual ways. You can stage a

bed-in in the comfort of your own home or travel to a fancy hotel for this delightful

activity, but regardless of the location, get ready for complete and total explora-

tion of each other, experimenting with new techniques.

Planning Your Getaway

Whether it's a hotel, motel, or vacation home rental, one thing is for sure: the bigger the bed, the better the bed-in! Be sure to ask for a king-size bed to give you enough room for maneuvering, experimenting, and relaxing!

- Book a five-star resort or hotel. One of the great pleasures of spending time in a five-star hotel is having sex in a really good bed.

- Look for hotels with "specially designed beds," such as the Hilton Garden Inn and its "Garden Sleep System," a bed that provides what's billed as "pressure-free" support and can be made soft or firm via controls. The Radisson Hotels & Resorts offer "Sleep Number" beds that let you customize the level of support or firmness. Visit http://hiltongardeninn1.hilton.com or www.radissonsleep numberbed.com for more information.

- Find an inn, a hotel, or a motel with waterbeds. Use the Internet to find locations near you.

- Search for hotels with unusual or themed beds, such as the FantaSuite chain of hotels in the Midwest. The Arabian Nights room features a 7-foot round bed surrounded by sheik's tent drapery, the Cave room features a 10-sided bed set in a cavelike setting, and the Space Odyssey room includes a bed set inside a recreation of the Gemini Space Capsule. Visit www.fantasuite.com for more information.

Packing for Pleasure

Be sure to pack getaway clothes and toiletries as well as these sexy additions:

- New pajamas for both of you: close-fitting cotton at the very least, and preferably silk

- Candles

- Handcuffs (and the keys to get out of them)

- Food and drinks for the weekend

- Reading material, games, and, of course, lubrication, condoms, or sex toys

- Drinking straws and popcorn (don't worry, I'll explain)

Friday

What usually happens by the time you get home from work on Friday night? Shoes off, feet up, some takeout, and then you're fast asleep. Not this weekend.

make a sexy bed

If you plan to conduct your bed-in at home, consider these tips for turning an ordinary mattress into a pleasure den worthy of a weekend stay:

- Make the bed with the highest quality sheets you can find (e.g., 300-count plush, silk, etc.), plush blankets, and a feather duvet.

- Buy some new pillows in all sizes, and in a variety of styles, from super soft to extra firm. Snuggling among pillows can make you feel like you're living on clouds!

- Choose the color of your décor, sheets, and duvet carefully: orange stimulates conversation, blue is calming, and red can heat things up! Alternatively, linens in neutral colors can be soothing to the eye and instantly relaxing.

- Don't forget the lighting and the scents. Surround yourself with romantic lighting and candles, sprinkle lavender under the pillows, or spritz your sheets with your favorite perfume.

- Stock the bedside table (and/or drawers) with water, sensual snacks, reading material, games, and, of course, lubrication, condoms, or sex toys!

- Add some personal and thoughtful touches—a framed picture of your lover, a new pair of slippers, a cozy robe, his favorite magazines, and so on.

- Don't forget trays for eating in bed!

HEAD TO BED

Do not turn the TV on as soon as you get home, because once it's on, it's over. Instead, turn on some music and light some candles. Your focus will be on your partner without any commercial breaks. And agree to the following ground rules:

1. Unless you are a doctor or on emergency call, no checking email, your PDA, or your pager.

2. Let the answering machine pick up your calls, and check them only at the end of the evening, if you must.

3. Absolutely no television, unless it's an adult or romantic movie with no commercial breaks.

Tonight's activity will be to focus on your shared bed, a shared meal, and a shared experience of love.

First, make your dinner and take it to the bedroom. Instead of just picking up the fork and digging in, feed each other and take time to indulge slowly. Being fed by your lover makes everything taste sweeter. (Avoid foods that are saucy, crumbly, or flaky—you don't want to spend the night whisking things out of bed or cleaning up spills!) When your dinner is over, it's time to clear everything away and engage in foreplay without touching each other.

- Stroke each other's hair and stare into each other's eyes.

- Recount your dreams with each other.

- Hold hands and entwine your legs.

- Lie on your partner's chest and listen to his/her heartbeat.

- Remove all your clothes and gently trail your fingers down your lover's arms and chest.

- Circle your partner's nipples with your fingers in slow motions.

- Outline your lover's lips with the tip of your finger.

Share a bedtime "bed" story with your lover. Ask your man if he ever snuck under his sheets as a kid with a flashlight and the magazines he found in his parents' bedroom. Guys, ask what girls' slumber parties are like and what girls talk about.

Beds are where we dream, so share a dream that you have for you and your lover: a daydream fantasy of something you'd love to do, or a place you long to go, or a way you want you and your lover to be. Becoming intimate in this way is a great way to finish the day, and a perfect prelude for more fun tomorrow!

Last but not least, have some fun with the popcorn and drinking straws! Lie on your backs, in bed. One of you take a straw, place a popped popcorn kernel on one end, blow it up into the air, and try to get it into your partner's mouth. You will be laughing so hard, any pressure or tension will melt like butter. Laughter gets your blood circulating and makes you more relaxed with your partner, both of which set the stage for snuggling.

Saturday

Today is the day for you to do as you please, in your bed. Catch up on reading that novel, flip through the newspaper, or better yet, do a crossword puzzle or Sudoku together. Make your bedroom your home base of operations for the day.

You don't have to stay *in* bed all day, but the point is to spend the weekend with your partner doing things you enjoy, with no emphasis on chores or work. So if you want to do some exercise (yoga or aerobics), do it in the bedroom. If you want to write some letters or make entries in your journal, do it in bed. If you and your partner want to lie horizontally, head to foot and foot to head, to give each other foot massages, do it in bed.

Of course, a nice way to start a Saturday morning is . . .

MORNING SEX

Morning sex is especially beneficial because men often wake up with an erection, and in a lot of cases, they are harder in the morning than they are if they get aroused at night. For women, it may take a little longer to get heated up in the morning, but that's where last night's snuggling comes in handy.

Try these maneuvers for morning lovin':

- Begin in the spoon/cuddle position with the man behind the woman, legs slightly bent.

- Men, wet one finger and place it inside her, slightly wiggling as you enter to make sure she is ready to go.

- With your wet finger, stroke her clitoris in small circles to get her further aroused.

- Pull her hips into you and introduce your penis between her legs.

- Move into her, but without being all the way inside her. Tease her entrance with your full erection.

- Hold up her leg and enter her slowly.

- Once inside, push all the way in, letting her accommodate your every inch.

- Stay inside her and slowly pulse your hips into her with slow and short movements.

- As you feel her respond, start pumping harder, adjusting her leg to suit both of you and grabbing on to her hips to guide her.

- Ladies, reach around and grab your partner's butt, pulling it into you according to how hard you want him to pulse.

- Move your hips in tune and also in opposition to his.

- Reach down to your labia and feel his penis inside you.

- Wet your fingers and moisten your clit for added pleasure.

Sex Positions to Keep You in Bed

You won't want to leave the bedroom once you dig into these spicy options!

- Go with the man on top, but ladies, try it with your head hanging over the edge of the bed. This kinky position changes your breathing pattern and intensifies sexual arousal. Just be careful if you feel lightheaded. You don't want to be in this position too long and let all the blood rush to your head.

- Want some G-spot love? Try having the man stand on the floor and the woman kneel at the edge of the bed, facing away from him. As he enters you from behind, your G-spot will be super stimulated and you can alternate between being upright or bending all the way forward. Changing the feel of his penetration helps stimulate all areas of your vagina. The more you move, the better it feels. (**See above.**)

- Want to be a little more adventurous? Try having the man lie with his back on the bed, but with his legs up on the wall. Ladies, sit on top of him with your back to the wall and pump up and down. Lean forward for more clit stimulation, backward for more G-spot action. As you control the movements, you can also try spinning around and alternating the center of pleasure to suit your desire. (**See right.**)

- Ladies, put your back against one wall and have your man stand between your legs as your hoist them both up against the opposite wall or wrap them around his thighs. He can help hold you up by your ass. Get ready for some deep penetration. For more excitement, try it handcuffed! **(See right.)**

- Men, give your lady oral sex with a flat tongue. As you build her up closer to orgasm, create pulses on her clitoris, varying the pressure according to how her body responds. Place one finger into her vagina, and when you feel pulses, clenching, or increased wetness, you know you're close to making her come. **(See below.)**

- Ladies, make him your main course, but ask him (if you don't already know) exactly what he likes best, and then do it! Many men like their testicles gently squeezed while you circle the tip of the penis; others enjoy deep throating. Go for a long lick from his balls up to the tip, and then take him fully into your mouth as far as you can go. Grasp the base, and as you move your mouth up, let your hand follow. Repeat!

ACKNOWLEDGMENTS

Hans, my husband, encouraged me to take on writing this book. And why wouldn't he? He seriously benefited from all the sexplay I had to test out before I put it to paper. Thank you, Hans, for your endless support, strong thighs, juicy lips, and oh-so-naughty mind. You inspire me. To my parents, who have been so supportive of my career writing about sex—your openness, acceptance, and unwavering love means the world to me. My sister has always lived by the mantras to do what you love, always go for it, and don't be afraid to start at the bottom and work your way up—she has helped infuse that mindset in me. Thank you. Big hug to Jamye Waxman for introducing me to this opportunity and having such a sexy voice—I've been your biggest fan since the beginning. Thanks to Arthur Nersesian, Margaret Atwood, and Sandra Cisneros—people I only know from reading their books, getting lost in their narrative, and making me realize writing is my passion. To Jill Alexander at Quiver for being so easy to talk to and offering me such insightful advice. To Fleetwood Mac and Bob Dylan for making such great music to type to. Thanks to the massage therapists who dutifully worked out the kinks in my neck from sitting at my desk for so many hours at a time. And thank you to the editors and everyone at Quiver, who made sure all the right kinks stood out in this book.

ABOUT THE AUTHOR

Michele Zipp is a former editor-in-chief of *Playgirl* magazine. She has written for various lifestyle publications both in print and online, and has authored erotic fiction that has been published in numerous anthologies. She currently is an editor at CafeMom, where she writes about parenting, beauty, style, sex, and relationships. Michele is a firm believer in truth, kink, respect, pedicures, fancy panties, chocolate, and her husband and family. She looks forward to reliving every chapter of this book.